A Mathematical Passage

A Mathematical Passage

STRATEGIES FOR PROMOTING INQUIRY IN GRADES 4–6

DAVID J. WHITIN & ROBIN COX

HEINEMANN
Portsmouth, NH

Heinemann
A division of Reed Elsevier Inc.
361 Hanover Street
Portsmouth, NH 03801–3912
www.heinemann.com

Offices and agents throughout the world

© 2003 by David J. Whitin and Robin Cox

All rights reserved. No part of this book may be reproduced in any form or by any electronic or mechanical means, including information storage and retrieval systems, without permission in writing from the publisher, except by a reviewer, who may quote brief passages in a review.

The authors and publisher wish to thank those who have generously given permission to reprint borrowed material.

The cover image from *Counting on Frank* by Rod Clement is used by permission of publisher Robert Famighetti and Harper Collins Publishers, Australia.

Library of Congress Cataloging-in-Publication Data
Whitin, David Jackman, 1947–
    A mathematical passage : strategies for promoting inquiry in grades 4–6 / David J. Whitin, Robin Cox.
       p.   cm.
    ISBN 0-325-00506-0 (pbk. : alk. paper)
    1. Mathematics—Study and teaching (Elementary). 2. Mathematics—Study and teaching (Middle school).   3. Inquiry (Theory of knowledge).   4. Questioning.
I. Cox, Robin.   II. Title.
QA135.6.W48   2003
372.7—dc21
                                                                              2003007291

Editor: Victoria Merecki
Production: Lynne Reed
Cover design: Jenny Jensen Greenleaf
Typesetter: House of Equations, Inc.
Manufacturing: Steve Bernier

Printed in the United States of America on acid-free paper
07 06 05 04 03   RRD   1 2 3 4 5

To Phyllis, who makes my passage through life so joyous.

—David

*To the students and to David, whom I had the privilege to work with
and learn from—thank you for making teaching rewarding.
To Andrew and Abigail, my precious children,
I am thankful for your curiosity and desire to learn.
You have my heart.
Most important, to Steve, my supportive and
loving husband—my life is blessed because of you. I love you.*

—Robin

Contents

Introduction 1

        Looking at Beliefs in the Mathematics Community 3

Chapter 1   Understanding the Classroom: An Interview with the Teacher 6

Chapter 2   Mathematicians Keep Records and Pose Their Own Problems 22

        The Investigation Begins 23

        Generating and Pursuing New Questions 25

        Reflecting on the Process 33

        What We Learned About the Process of Inquiry 33

        Going Beyond the Experience 34

Chapter 3   Mathematicians Are Skeptics Who Go Beyond the Data 36

        The Investigation Begins 37

        Discussing Our Findings 39

        Skepticism Leads to Further Investigating 41

        Mathematicians Go Beyond the Data 45

        Mathematicians Create Their Own Language 50

        Going Beyond the Experience 53

Chapter 4   Mathematicians Are Problem Solvers Who Invent Their Own Tools 55

        Starting the Investigation 57

	The First Day: Examining the Potato and the Squash	57
	Developing Tools for Calculating the Area	62
	Testing Their Measuring Tools	66
	A Window into One Child's Thinking	67
	Calculating the Area Using Water	69
	Using Clay to Determine Area	71
	Summarizing Our Findings	76
	Going Beyond the Experience	77
Chapter 5	Mathematicians Discover Patterns and Relationships	80
	The Initial Investigation	80
	The First Conversation: Mathematicians Analyze Patterns and Develop Theories	84
	Teachers Are Vulnerable Too: Reflecting on What We Did Not Know	91
	Conjectures About Patterns Build a Sense of Community	92
	Children Reflect on the Conversation	94
	The Strength of Triangles: Mathematicians Connect Concepts to the Real World	95
	Building Structures of Their Own: Mathematicians Apply Their New Knowledge	97
	Children Reflect on Working Together	100
	Investigating the Strength of Structures	102
	Examining the Buildings of Others	104
	Reflecting on the Experience with Triangles	106
	Going Beyond the Experience	106
	Notes: Clarification from a University Colleague	107
Chapter 6	Developing a Math Workshop	109
	Laying the Groundwork for the Math Workshop	111
	Pursuing Heartbeats, Deaths, and Nanoseconds	115
	Exploring the Largest Potato Chip and the Largest Stamp	119

How Long Does It Take a Jet to Go Around the World? 120
Investigating the Fort McHenry Flag 124
Counting to One Million 126
Other Math Workshop Explorations 129
Teachers' Reflections on Math Workshop: Benefits and
Next Steps 131
Children's Reflections on the Benefits of Math Workshop 133

Chapter 7 Reflections on Living a Mathematical Life 136
A Conversation with Jason 137
A Mathematician's Bill of Rights 139

References 141

A Mathematical Passage

Introduction

Books get written because writers have questions. This book is no exception. Teaching is a journey, and as such, it is never easy, never well marked, and never over. In fact, teaching is inquiry, and the closer we look at what we do as teachers, the more questions we have about what to do next. Feeling a bit unsettled comes with the territory. Part of this uneasiness is what brought the two of us together—classroom teacher Robin Cox and university teacher David Whitin.

Both of us had questions about our teaching. Of course, this is not to say that we were not pleased with some of what we had done in the past. Robin felt good about the writer's workshop that she had developed in her classroom, where children had choices about and ownership for their writing. She had worked hard to incorporate literature throughout the curriculum. She incorporated a range of mathematical manipulatives in her program to help her students understand, and not just memorize, mathematical skills, concepts, and strategies. She involved her children in numerous hands-on experiences in the areas of science and social studies. She worked very hard to build a sense of community in her room where students respected each other's feelings and ideas. David, too, was pleased with some of his recent accomplishments in the classroom. He had worked with classroom teacher Tim O'Keefe and fellow university collaborator Heidi Mills in his first- and second-grade classrooms. He had gained many insights about learning from this collaborative work: the importance of children writing their own mathematical stories; the ability of young children to collect and display data in their own way; the power of children's literature to demonstrate mathematical thinking in meaningful contexts (Whitin, Mills, and O'Keefe 1990; Mills, O'Keefe, and Whitin 1996).

However, we each had questions about our teaching, especially in the area of mathematics. Robin saw the excitement that her children displayed when they had choices in writing their own stories and reading books (during a silent sustained reading time). She wanted to nurture this same kind of ownership in the area of mathematics. How could she begin to offer choice in math? How could children develop more ownership for the mathematics they were exploring? How could she use what she knew about language learning to help her make this transition? David had questions as well. How could he support older children in developing more ownership for their mathematical thinking? How could he use his previous work with younger children to help him in his work with older students? These were some of the nagging questions that brought the two of us together.

We were also drawn together by our common interest in effective principles of language learning. We were both members of a teacher support group that met once a month to discuss educational issues. The group read teacher-resource books together, discussed effective strategies for reading and writing instruction, and shared the latest children's books with each other. On one occasion our group read together a teacher-resource book on inquiry learning (Watson, Burke, and Harste 1989). This book, and our discussion about its key ideas, had a major influence on how we thought about working together. In this book the authors describe five conditions for inquiry (p. 12):

1. Teacher and student accept vulnerability and see it as a necessary part of real learning.
2. Teacher and student experience a sense of real community in their learning.
3. Teacher and student insist that their learning be generative; that is, it must lead to further insights, connections, and action.
4. Teacher and student demand democracy, insisting that all voices be heard.
5. Teacher and student recognize that inquiry is reflexive; they see themselves and each other as instruments for their own learning.

During our discussion of this book our teacher support group framed these conditions as questions and brainstormed strategies for supporting their growth in the classroom. It is important to share some of the group's ideas because these became the basis of the collaboration between the two of us.

1. How can we develop an environment that encourages learners to share their vulnerability?
    a. Encourage multiple interpretations of an event.
    b. Value tentativeness, uncertainty, being unsure.
    c. Support children in sharing unanticipated results.
    d. Foster a spirit of risk taking.
    e. Respect and nurture difference in all that children do.
2. How do we develop a sense of community in the classroom?
    a. Recognize students as teachers, and teachers as students.
    b. Give students a voice in curriculum investigations.

c. Develop experiences that recognize individual talent and group potential.

   d. Establish a sharing time for students to discuss their work.

3. How do we develop an environment that fosters the generation of knowledge?

   a. Provide students with multiple ways to express their ideas.

   b. Demonstrate that questions often lead to further questions.

   c. Recognize how our peers help us generate new ideas.

4. How do we develop an environment in which all voices are heard?

   a. Provide open-ended activities.

   b. Focus conversations on the process of how children solve problems.

   c. Value children's questions.

   d. Share literature that celebrates different voices.

5. How do we develop an environment that encourages learners to be reflexive?

   a. Encourage children to represent and retell their problem-solving strategies.

   b. Support children in revising their initial ideas.

   c. Ask children to evaluate their own efforts.

As Robin and I discussed the idea of working together we returned to these ideas. Robin wanted to find out what these ideas looked like from a mathematical perspective. She had worked hard to support these conditions in the areas of reading and writing but wanted to know more about how to nurture these ideas in her mathematics instruction. David was also interested in looking more closely at how to build an inquiring mathematics classroom, especially in the upper elementary grades. He found that as he shared his work with younger children, he was often asked by other teachers, "How would you go about teaching this way with older students who have more difficult math to master?" Somehow the notion had developed that teaching older students would be different. A collaboration with Robin would broaden David's experience and help him answer these questions about older learners.

Looking at Beliefs in the Mathematics Community

One of the ways we began to make some connections between these conditions of inquiry and mathematics was to examine publications by National Council of Teachers of Mathematics (NCTM) that described their beliefs about teaching and learning. For example, in the *Professional Standards for Mathematics Teaching* (NCTM 1991, p. 3), we discovered a vision of school mathematics that emphasized understanding, invention, and sense making. This vision advocated a shift in teaching and learning mathematics:

toward classrooms as mathematics communities	away from classrooms as simply a collection of individuals
toward logic and mathematical evidence as verification	away from the teacher as the sole authority for the right answers
toward mathematical reasoning	away from merely memorizing procedures
toward conjecturing, inventing, and problem solving	away from an emphasis on mechanistic finding of answers
toward connecting mathematics, its ideas, and its applications	away from treating mathematics as a body of isolated concepts and procedures

We saw that the mathematics community also sought to build classroom environments in which children are active constructors of their knowledge. NCTM's *Curriculum and Evaluation Standards for School Mathematics* (NCTM 1989) used verbs that help define what it means to think mathematically: explore, investigate, conjecture, solve, justify, represent, formulate, discover, construct, verify, explain, predict, develop, describe, and use. We knew that making this kind of thinking a reality did not just happen, but was a product of an environment that valued individual voices, promoted risk taking, and made thinking the currency of conversation (Hiebert 1997).

One of the most significant parts of NCTM's *Curriculum and Evaluation Standards for School Mathematics* (1989) is its goals for students. These same five goals are embedded in the revised *Principles and Standards for School Mathematics* (2000, pp. 5–6):

1. Learn to value mathematics.
2. Become confident in one's ability to do mathematics.
3. Become mathematical problem solvers.
4. Learn to communicate mathematics.
5. Learn to reason mathematically.

We realized that these worthy goals would be realized only in a community that respected each person's thinking, supported the active participation of all students, and allowed them to be reflective about their thinking. Thus, it was helpful for us to shift between the conditions of inquiry that we had discussed earlier and the vision of mathematics instruction advocated by NCTM. We needed both to give us a sense of direction and purpose.

The more we examined NCTM's standards documents (1989, 2000), the more we saw a parallel emphasis on building a community of inquirers. Drawing out individual voices and sharing one's vulnerability were key emphases in the standards. In fact, one of the process standards is "communication," in which students are expected to "feel free to express their ideas, explore mathematical ideas from multiple perspectives, and to justify solutions in the face of disagreement" (2000, pp. 60–61). It is an interesting irony that as students share their vulnerability (such as their uncertainty), they can become more confident in their mathematical thinking. However, this change can happen only in a supportive community in which students are "encouraged to explore, take risks, share failures and successes, and question one another" (2000, p. 53).

Developing an environment that fosters the generation of knowledge is described in the NCTM standards in several ways. First, it is important for students to generate their own "everyday, familiar language" to articulate their mathematical understanding (2000, p. 63). NCTM's caveat is to "avoid a premature rush to impose formal mathematical language" (2000, p. 63). Another aspect of generating knowledge involves making connections (another process standard), not only among mathematical topics and concepts, but also to applications in the real world. Another process standard, representation, advocates that students generate multiple forms of representation so that they can "construct, refine, and use their own representations as tools to support learning and doing mathematics" (2000, p. 68).

Given our readings about inquiry learning and the mathematics goals of NCTM, we were able to outline our purpose of working together: to encourage children to do what mathematicians do in the context of an inquiring community. We have organized the book chapters around some of the principal activities of mathematicians: keep records, pose their own problems, assume a skeptical stance, go beyond the data, seek patterns, and develop theories. In the context of this mathematical work is a description of the classroom values that made such work possible. These values were to promote a sense of community, encourage risk-taking, develop a democratic attitude, and foster the generation of knowledge as well as a reflective stance.

1 Understanding the Classroom: An Interview with the Teacher

Robin taught a heterogeneous fifth-grade class in a middle-class suburban neighborhood. She chose to be self-contained (i.e., to teach all subjects herself) even though the other fifth-grade teachers rotated for mathematics and science instruction. Robin felt being self-contained gave her students more extended periods of time for investigations and conversations in mathematics (and other subject areas). She addressed district goals and objectives in mathematics that she was expected to follow and used the traditional mathematics textbook she was given. However, Robin supplemented this textbook with many works of children's literature and a wide range of manipulatives that included base 10 blocks, pattern blocks, geoboards, and tiles. She knew the district goals in math but used the textbook in a flexible way so that she could better meet the needs of her students. She would often introduce a mathematical topic with a piece of literature or a problem involving manipulatives, and then use the textbook as homework for additional practice.

We begin this book with an interview with Robin because we know it is the teacher, and that person's beliefs about learning, that influences all that happens in a classroom. In this chapter, Robin discusses in greater depth what she feels are important features of good mathematics instruction. Her description of her classroom provides important background information so that you can better understand and appreciate the classroom stories that follow in the remaining chapters. In this interview Robin discusses numerous ideas:

- How she manages her time to meet the needs of all her students
- How she meets district guidelines in mathematics
- How she addresses certain math topics throughout the year
- How she supplements her math textbook with manipulatives, literature, and real-world applications
- How she develops strategies for building a community of learners
- How she uses math journals
- How she communicates with parents about her math program

- How she views mathematical learning from an inquiry perspective

With these ideas in mind, consider Robin's thoughts on her classroom, her children, and her beliefs about mathematical learning.

1. Since you teach all subjects, how do you organize your day, and how does mathematics fit into your busy schedule?

I think the best way to start is to share my daily schedule.

Mrs. Cox's Fifth-Grade Class Daily Schedule

7:30–8:05:	Students arrive, unpack, submit notes, lunch money, signed papers, parent journals, etc. Students begin on morning choices. Students participate in a variety of instructional activities, such as independent reading, math manipulatives, math journals, and writers' notebooks.
8:05–8:10:	"Live on Five"—schoolwide televised program
8:10–8:25:	Morning choices • Calendar (base 5 and base 10) • *Counting on Frank* journal sharing • "This Day in History" • Student sharing (students sign up to share items related to current topics of study) • Share class forecast for the day (what we have planned for the day) • Chapter book read-aloud
8:25–10:15:	Reading and writing workshops

Reading and Writing Workshop Typical Schedule

8:25–8:45:	Independent reading and conferences
8:45–8:55:	Reading minilesson
8:55–9:20:	Student reading—students participate in literature study groups, small-group guided reading, and research of inquiry topics (this varies depending on our current inquiry in social studies or science as well as student interests)
9:20–9:30:	Sharing—debriefing strategies, ideas, "aha's"
9:30–9:40:	Minilesson
9:40–10:05:	Student writing—participating in writing workshop, research and writing about inquiry topics, occasional class writing projects such as fraction stories
10:05–10:15:	Sharing

Note: Word study is integrated into the reading and writing workshop (e.g., use of prefix, suffix, and root words to understand reading vocabulary, to improve writing, etc.). Spelling was individualized—students, with teacher input, selected ten words per week from their writing (and word study if needed) to learn. Students had spelling buddies for testing and other activities.

10:15–11:05: Related arts (art, music, physical education, media center, computer lab)
11:05–11:35: Inquiry time (social studies)
11:35–11:55: Lunch
11:55–12:15: Recess
12:20–1:20: Math
1:20–2:10: Science
2:10–2:15: Review the day and homework assignments; pack up
2:15: Dismissal of bus riders and car riders
2:25: Dismissal of walkers

2. Can you talk more specifically about how you organized your math program and how you addressed the needs of your students?

Like any teacher, I was responsible for covering the required skills and concepts for my grade. I had to give my principal my instructional goals for each subject every six weeks. These plans reflected the mandated curriculum that my district had developed. The following year-long plan is an outline of the goals that I submitted for mathematics during one year.

Mathematics Year-Long Plan: Robin Cox, Fifth Grade

1st Six Weeks

Concepts of number (Ch. 31): Base 3, 4, 5, 6

Other numeration systems and history of mathematics (Chs. 1 and 31)

Whole numbers (Ch. 2): Recognize names for numbers, place value, compare and order numbers

2nd Six Weeks

Multiplication (Chs. 5 and 15)

Division (Chs. 6 and 16)

Student-generated projects, such as sports: Address statistics and probability, percent (Ch. 23), averaging

3rd Six Weeks

Measurement and geometry (Chs. 7, 8, 29): Architecture study

The meaning of fractions: Equivalence, partitioning (Chs. 9 and 10)

Student workshop projects: Address and review many mathematical concepts and skills

4th Six Weeks

Addition and subtraction of fractions (Ch. 11)

Multiplication of fractions (Chs. 12 and 19)

Meaning of fractions and percent

Student workshop projects: Address and review many mathematical concepts and skills

5th Six Weeks

Addition and subtraction of decimals (Ch. 20)

Multiplication of decimals (Ch. 21)

Addition and subtraction of fractions and mixed numbers (Chs. 26 and 27)

Student workshop projects: Address and review many mathematical concepts and skills

6th Six Weeks

Multiplication and division of mixed numbers and fractions (Ch. 25)

Percent (Ch. 23)

Integers (Ch. 30)

Student workshop projects: Address and review many mathematical concepts and skills

Note: Statistics, probability, graphing, measurement, and collecting and representing data are integrated all year.

Note to Administration Concerning Long-Range Plans

We address statistics, measurement (in addition to the third six-week period), probability, and collecting and representing data (graphing) throughout the year. The use of tools in mathematics such as computers and calculators is also addressed throughout the year. We examine the historical nature of mathematics so that children have a sense of its evolution and development. In addition, we use math journals as a tool for understanding and extending our thinking. These journals also serve as an assessment tool, as I make instructional decisions based on the students' understanding. They also help students learn to communicate their reasoning and thus develop mathematical power (NCTM 2000). Because I believe that math is a sign system—a means of communicating about our world—it is a natural part of our study of content areas and is integrated as we explore a variety of topics.

You can see in my daily schedule that I mention calendar time using bases 5 and 10. I use a different base for our calendar each month. I use base 10 of course, but I also use another base so that children have a sense for other numeration systems. You can buy blocks in different bases from ETA/Cuisenaire Company (www.etacuisenaire.com). I have bases 2 through 9 and use several of them throughout the year to tally the day of the month. The blocks are available for the children to use during math workshop or during our morning "settling-in" time. Examining different bases helps children learn important place value ideas; for example, there is a consistent grouping across a base system, and the value of a digit is determined by its place. We also keep track of the date using different numeration systems from other cultures, such as Babylonian, Egyptian, Mayan, Roman, and Chinese. Claudia Zaslavsky has written some helpful books for teachers that describe these different systems (1994, 1996).

I also supplement my math textbook with a wide range of math manipulatives: base 10 blocks, pattern blocks, fraction bars, Cuisenaire rods, geoboards, tiles (for building arrays in multiplication), and measuring tools. Mathematics can be abstract for children, but these manipulatives give students a model for visualizing the patterns and processes being discussed. Since my students often used manipulatives to solve computational problems, I did not require that they solve every problem in their math textbook. Instead, I had them use the blocks to solve ten problems (rather than twenty). The children and I referred to the textbook as "the math handbook." We used it as a handbook to help us when we had a question about a specific skill. I did give homework problems from the text, both computational and word problems. But I introduced many of the key concepts through manipulatives. For instance, I used base 10 blocks to introduce division and I used tiles to introduce building arrays in multiplication.

As the plan shows, some math topics I covered throughout the year, such as statistics, measurement, and probability. For instance, data collection and analysis could be naturally woven into almost any investigation. Children made charts to document the growth of seeds, to examine the population of the New England colonies, and to record their heart rate during a health unit. Mean, median, and mode were also required topics in the fifth grade. Therefore, I often had the children display their data in these different ways so they could see what relationships were revealed and concealed by each display. Measuring was another topic that I addressed throughout the year (although I did focus on certain measurement ideas during the third marking period). Children measured the growth of plants, determined perimeter and area of shapes during an architecture study, and discussed the passage of time almost every day as we told time by our classroom clock.

When I think of the math skills and concepts that my children must know in fifth grade, I try to plan in reverse. That is, I ask myself, "Why would someone need to know this in the real world? What is the point of teaching this skill/concept anyway?" Then I try to think of meaningful contexts for these skills and use them in my teaching. For instance, many students were interested in the World Series, so we looked at how baseball averages are determined.

I also provided time in my daily schedule for children to share writing that was part of our *Counting on Frank* journal. This story (Clement 1991) shows a child who creates mathematical ideas as he wanders around his living room, dining room, and backyard. He is a wonderer, imagining how many dogs it would take to fill up his bedroom, how long it would take him to fill his entire bathroom with water, or how tall he would be if he grew as fast as the gum tree in his yard. I like this story because it demonstrates what it means to view the world math-

Figure 1–1   The traveling doll and his journal

ematically. It is the concepts—such big ideas as equivalence, number, length, ratio, volume, capacity, probability, average, place value, symmetry, congruence, variable, and time—that enable us to do this kind of mathematical thinking. (Robin and David discussed these ideas frequently as they read *Mathematics in the Making* by Mills, O'Keefe, and Whitin 1996.) I want the children to realize that anyone can view the world mathematically.

I have used this story to encourage mathematical thinking outside the classroom. I asked my sister, who is a talented seamstress, to make a doll that looked like the little boy in *Counting on Frank* (Figure 1–1). I also gave the doll a journal and a backpack. I invited children to take the doll home and share him with their family. The only requirement was that the student had to record the doll's thoughts in the journal. We discussed the kind of mathematical thoughts that the boy expressed in the story. We challenged the children to record similar kinds of thinking as the doll accompanied them in their daily routines. Almost every child decided to take the doll home at some time during the year. Following are some excerpts from that journal that show how the children were using the doll as a mathematical filter for viewing their world.

AARON: I was shooting the basketball and I thought if I scored 12 points and 1 free throw in one game, and in the next game I scored 2 points and 2 free throws, how many points do I average a game?

BOBBY: On the way home everybody wanted to hold me, and that started me thinking: How many people in the world would like to hold me the first time they saw me?

JAKE: I wonder how many packs of Skittles you can fit into your mouth.

RICHIE: After TV Richie went to bed, and I heard Richie's sister snoring very, very loud. I wanted to know how many snores combined would break the decibel meter.

COLE: I saw a lot of people playing "Pickle." It got me thinking, how many people buy balls in the average year? One person asked, "Can I go the bathroom?" And that got me thinking, how many gallons are used in a day?

LAUREN: Today Lauren had a stomachache and a sore throat. Around 10:00 A.M. she started sneezing. That got me thinking, how many bacteria germs are in the average sneeze?

CHASE: His dad was adding up how many hours Chase had ridden on the horse. He has 500 hours. I wondered how long it had taken to ride that long.

Today we are going to his grandma's house. I wonder how many cars we will pass.

We had to get up early to come to school. I wonder how many people get up at this time?

HEDDA: Now Hedda is eating a blow-pop. I wonder how many licks will it take to get to the bubble-gum part.

Now we are jumping from bed to bed like monkeys. I wonder how high the average person jumps.

Wow! Now Hedda is talking on the phone with Leslie. I wonder if they talk 3 hours a day, how much will they talk in one year.

MELISSA: When I was picking honey sickles I asked myself, "How many honey sickles are there in a patch?"

When eating pizza I asked myself, "If I had 50 large pizzas, how many slices would that be?

When doing my homework, I was wondering how many people forget their homework in one day.

So, this traveling doll was one way that I fostered a mathematical view of the world.

3. How did you meet the needs of all your students in math?

One strategy was having children work in rotation all day. The following table shows a daily schedule of rotations.

I created this schedule out of a need to work intensively with a small group in math. I have found that I can accomplish a lot if I give myself a concentrated period of time with a small group of children. I can get each one involved and can answer their individual questions. For example, when I first introduced division, I wanted to have forty-five minutes of concentrated time to work with the children—to fully immerse them in the learning activity I had planned for them. I also used this time to address common math difficulties. For instance, some children were confusing mean, median, and mode. On another occasion some children needed help in multiplying a one-digit number by a two-digit number. I used

Sample Daily Schedule of Rotations

	Group 1	Group 2	Group 3	Group 4	Group 5
8:25–9:15	Math small group	Science experiment	Independent reading	Social studies activity	Writing workshop
9:15–10:00	Writing workshop	Math small group	Science experiment	Independent reading	Social studies activity
10:00–10:45	Social studies activity	Writing workshop	Math small group	Science experiment	Independent reading
10:45–11:35			Related arts		
11:35–12:20			Lunch and recess		
12:20–1:10	Independent reading	Social studies activity	Writing workshop	Math small group	Science experiment
1:10–1:55	Science experiment	Independent reading	Social studies activity	Writing workshop	Math small group
1:55–2:10			Debrief the day—Where do we need to go from here?		

Here is a sample day's activities:

Math group—Working with me on division; moving from manipulatives to paper.
Science experiment—Dissecting several seeds and labeling them using the diagram in the textbook.
Independent reading—Completing specific assignments with their literature books.
Social studies activity—Reading a section from the textbook and writing a running conversation with the text.
Writing workshop—Working on writing in progress. If someone needed a conference with me, they had to wait until the next day. They had other writing options, such as write a note to a friend, post a note on the message board, or write their pen pal.

this time just as I did my writing workshop time, when I would meet with small groups of children and help them understand, for instance, how alliteration worked or how to take research notes from a textbook. It was a time to cluster kids together who needed individualized help with a specific skill. While I was meeting with a group, the other children rotated to different activities.

Some readers may be wondering how well the children worked independently and whether I had any classroom management problems. I truly did not, but note that I did not start this rotating schedule until we were approximately four weeks into school. I first had to establish a sense of community. I had to plan experiences that would highlight the norms of our living together as a classroom community. The other point is that I did not use this schedule on a weekly basis; it was utilized maybe twice a month at most. Another key to designing a successful rotation is to make sure that students in the small groups know exactly what to do and that the activities do not require the teacher's intervention or assistance. I also positioned myself strategically in the room so I could see all activities. I would periodically make a quick sweep of the room as the children in my small group worked out a problem with the manipulatives.

I tried to use any free moment that I had to address the needs of my students— even during a recess time or before school. As strange as it may seem, the kids did not mind missing a few minutes (or more) of recess to meet with me. They did not see our meetings as punishment, but rather as a time for learning and understanding. I think part of their attitude came from the sense of community that we were building. They knew that one of the things that made us a close classroom "family" (a word I often used) was that we helped each other. The other reason that they willingly met with me is that much of their work (including their math work) was to be shared with their peers, and they wanted it right. I have found that when children have an audience for their work they develop a sense of ownership and responsibility for their finished products.

4. You mentioned that you worked hard to build a sense of community. What strategies did you use to foster the development of this community?

To start the year I read several picture books about quilt making to the students. For me the quilt was a metaphor for teamwork. It represented the blending together of individual talents and strengths, just as different patches of material merge to make something beautiful. We would talk about our class as a patchwork of personalities who have unique gifts to share. I was always on the lookout for ways to highlight the talents of my children. I was especially eager to recognize the strengths of my special education students as well as draw out the voices of the girls in the class. Once I got to know the girls I would call on them directly even if their hands were not raised because I knew that they had important ideas to share.

Another strategy that I used to build a sense of community at the beginning of the year was to invite the children to do "Expert Projects." Each child was to select a topic that he or she knew a lot about and develop a report on that topic for the rest of the class. Children chose horseback riding, cross-stitching, jets, and so on. I wanted the children to appreciate the unique talents of each of their classmates. Brandi was the person who reported on jets, and I made a point of telling the class that "there are no projects that are just for boys or girls. Brandi liked jets so she reported on jets, and she didn't think that was a topic just for boys." Later on in the year Derek investigated the speed of jets during math workshop time, and he relied on Brandi for advice. Another thing I insisted on from the very beginning of the year: Boys and girls work together in this room. Sometimes children chose whom they would work with on group projects and sometimes I chose the groups. I always mixed girls and boys. We talked about the importance of working together with different people and how we can learn from each other. Because I believe in the social nature of learning I would often have the children reflect on how well they worked with their partner(s). We shared strategies for working together as well as tips for overcoming roadblocks. You will read about many of these reflections in this book.

Another strategy for building a sense of community is that problems were fixed and decisions were made by the group, and not by me. The issue could be as mundane as, "Where are good places in the room to work on your math project?" Or it might be of a more serious matter: "How can we make Melissa feel better now that her feelings have been hurt?" By giving this kind of responsibility to the class I was also giving them a sense of ownership for its evolution and development.

Another thing I work on at the beginning of the year is how the children can talk to each other in a respectful manner. I want my students to think and question, but they must do so in a way that does not undermine our community. At the beginning of the year I say to my students, "In this classroom you can challenge and disagree with the ideas of your classmates. You have that right, and it is part of being a mathematical thinker. However, I expect you to do it in a way that respects your classmate's thinking. I will not tolerate people making fun of another person's ideas, or trying to make themselves look better than another person. How do you suppose you can challenge another person's ideas in a respectful way?" The children then brainstorm possible responses, such as:

- I have a slightly different idea than Cole . . .
- I agree with part of Michael's idea but I disagree with another part . . .
- I understand what Stephanie is saying but I thought about the problem in another way . . .

Together the students and I create a list of acceptable responses for disagreeing. (Students can also role-play each phrase using both respectful and sarcastic tones of voice to show how the same words can convey very different meanings.)

5. You had your children keep math journals. What was the purpose of these journals? How did you use them?

I had kids keep math journals because I wanted a place for them to record their thinking and to reflect on what they were learning. I use a lot of manipulatives in my classroom, but these materials don't magically guarantee understanding. So as children worked with manipulatives, I expected them to record their thoughts in their journals. I encouraged them to write, draw, make charts, and so on to express their understanding. I always provided time for some children to share their entries each day so that we could all see how different students used their journals.

Their writing gave me a window into their thinking. They would write in their journals almost every day, and I would read their entries that night. Their writing helped me plan what to do next. For instance, if I saw that some children did not seem to understand place value in division, I would make a note of that. I would meet with that group of students, or pair them up with other students during the next activity. Journals helped me assess children's understanding, and that is what my math program is all about. Right answers are important, but if they come at the expense of understanding I am very concerned. I keep telling my students that we are a "thinking class" and the journals are one way for them to express their thinking. I also tell them my intentions directly: "The reason we keep math journals is that they provide a place for you to share your thinking. I want you to understand what you are learning, because if you understand it, you can use it to solve other problems." I think children, especially older children, need to know that I, as a teacher, am making deliberate decisions about their options as learners. I tell them, "Learning is not an option, but how we learn is." I tell them that I have structured the classroom so that they have different options for expressing what they know. I encourage them to keep asking themselves, "Is this making sense to me?" and to use that sense making as a focus for their journal writing.

One of the things that I encouraged the children to do throughout the year was to record lingering questions in their journals. We came to refer to these lingerings as "wonders." I found that these wonders often helped me see what children did not understand and provided the next steps in my planning. By the way, the word "wonder" was first used by one of my students, Tanya. Several weeks after school started she wrote, "I wonder . . ." in her journal, followed by several different investigations that she wanted to pursue with different base block materials. I liked the connotation that this new word seemed to carry with it—a yearning to know. I used to ask kids to write down any questions they had in their journals. That prompt never seemed to work very well. But when we replaced the word *question* with *wonder*, the difference in their responses was dramatic. This one word seemed to open them up in a less threatening way. When we asked them about this change, they said that *wonder* reminded them of "exploring" and "doing research." We suspected that *question* carried with it a past association of not being "smart" in math, or not paying attention to what the teacher said. So you'll see the word *wonder* throughout this book.

I'll share with you some of their "wonders" during our investigation with fractions. This will give you a better understanding of how I used these journals. At the beginning of a unit on fractions I had asked the children to record their thoughts and wonders about fractions. Jason wrote about the similarity between fractions and division, and then wondered if fractions can exist in shapes other than circles (Figure 1–2). Notice that he extended his wondering to ask if fractions could be applied to three-dimensional shapes. His reflection helped me in my planning. I wanted to be sure that I exposed the children not only to an area model for fractions (such as the circle model that Jason refers to) but also to a set model of discrete objects, such as a set of eggs. Jason's comment also reminded me of the importance of having kids work with a variety of area models, such as fraction bars, pattern blocks, and Cuisenaire rods. Thus the journals inform me about Jason's narrow view of fractions (just circles), but they also cause me to reflect on my own teaching and make sure that I am broadening children's experiences with fractions. So the journals benefit the whole learning process—for both me and the students.

Here is one other example. Melissa, LaToya, and Jennifer recorded some other wonders as they were engaged in several fraction activities in class (Figure 1–3). Melissa wondered how many equivalent names a fraction can have, LaToya

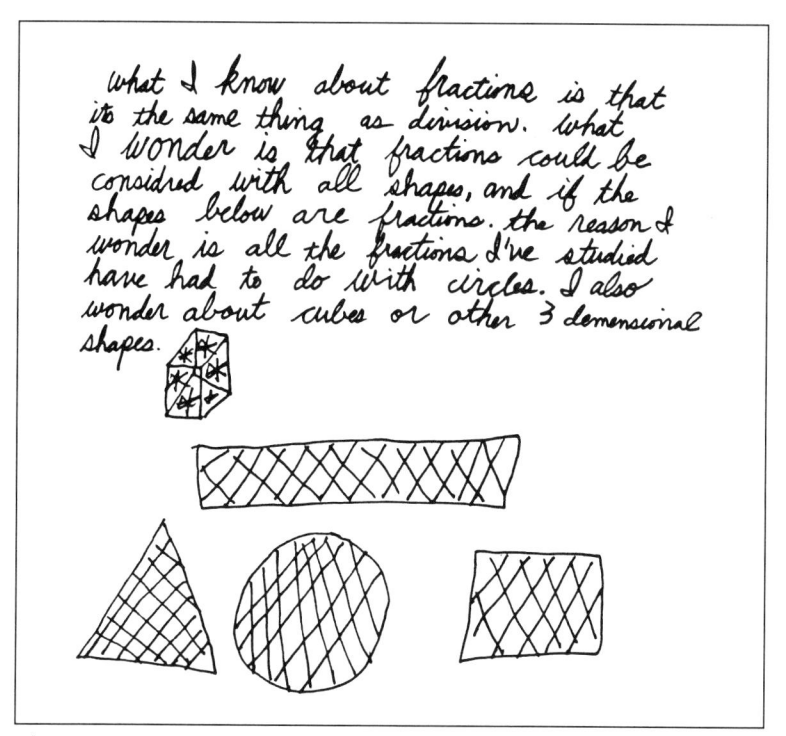

Figure 1–2

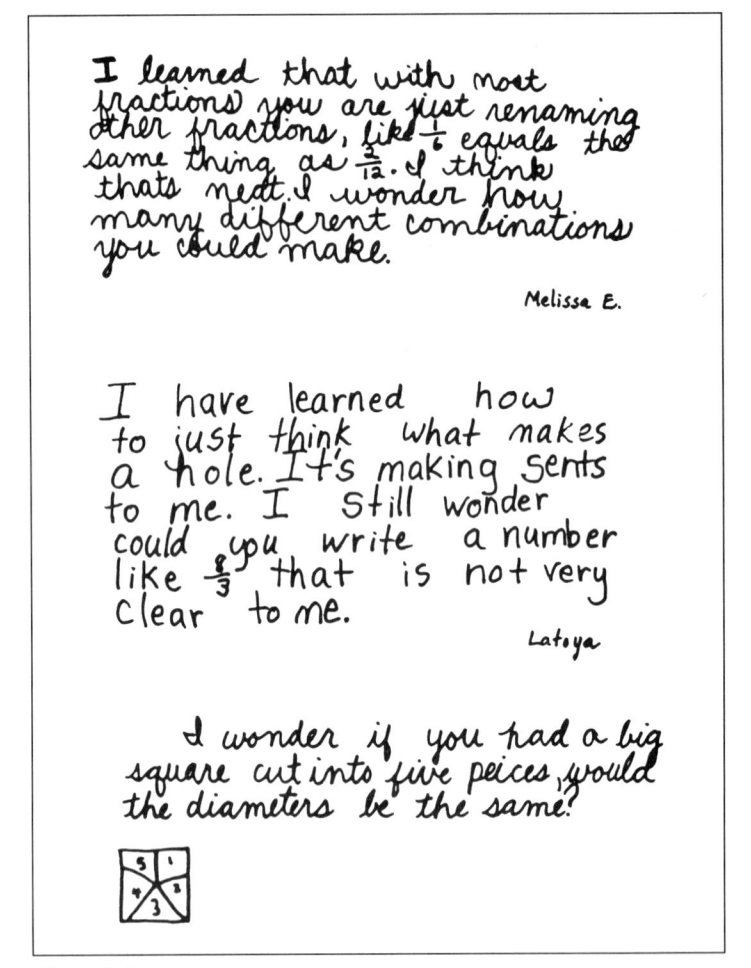

> I learned that with most fractions you are just renaming other fractions, like 1/6 equals the same thing as 2/12. I think thats neat. I wonder how many different combinations you could make.
>
> — Melissa E.

> I have learned how to just think what makes a hole. It's making sents to me. I still wonder could you write a number like 8/3 that is not very clear to me.
>
> — Latoya

> I wonder if you had a big square cut into five peices, would the diameters be the same?

Figure 1–3

wondered about the sense of having a numerator greater than a denominator, and Jennifer wondered about dividing a square into five equal pieces with lines that are the same length. Again, these wonders helped me in my planning. I decided to spend more time with fraction bars and a number line so we could explore equivalent fractions in greater depth. I also decided that I wanted the children to build and discuss more "improper" fractions so that they could make sense of what those numbers represented. I actually combined the first two wonders by having the children find many different names for 5/2. This wondering not only helped me in my planning but also did a lot to build a sense of community. Wondering is risky business for kids. It means admitting that you are not certain, and you have questions about ideas that you think you are "supposed to know." I worked hard to nurture this wondering by sharing these questions publicly. I would also comment to students directly about how we all benefit from each other's uncertainties.

6. How did you communicate with parents about this inquiry approach to math?

At the beginning of each school year we had an open house for parents. It was a time for us all to meet and a time for me to share my curriculum goals for the year. In math I stressed that I wanted their children to understand what they were learning. I gave them a list of the district math objectives for fifth grade. I said that my goal for their children was to understand these skills, and know how and when to use them. I mentioned that I used many materials to help kids visualize these concepts and to better see patterns and relationships. I would often show them base 10 blocks and briefly demonstrate how this model can help kids with their understanding of the place value system. I would mention how these blocks are also helpful in understanding the metric system, relating it to liters and cubic meters. I would mention the example of pi, and how many of us going through school only knew it as 3.14 but never understood where it came from. I would share how their children would be measuring circular objects to discover this ratio on their own. I have always found parents very receptive to this kind of instruction. They can relate to my emphasis on understanding because most of them went through school memorizing mathematical formulas and algorithms in a rote way. In fact, a common response from parents is, "Gosh, I wish I had had those materials when I was in school!"

Throughout the year I kept in constant contact with parents. I sent home a weekly newsletter that described the different topics that we were studying in all subjects. In math I would give my reasons for doing what I was doing. For instance, I would discuss the mathematical implications for our architecture unit. I would explain why we were studying a different numeration system each month. I wanted the parents to know very clearly what important mathematical ideas were being found in our investigations. I also kept parent journals. Each parent had a journal and we communicated each week in these journals. It was a way for me to say something specific about each child each week. Sometimes a parent would raise a question, such as, "Why does my child have only ten math problems to do for homework and not thirty?" I would respond to this parent but then include a similar question in the weekly newsletter so that all parents could better understand my intentions. The newsletter and the journals gave the parents a voice in my classroom. Several parents often said to me, "I knew I could always come to you if I had a question." I could better support the growth of each child if I had the support of their parents.

7. What are some of the key ideas about learning mathematics through inquiry? How are these ideas featured in this book?

I developed a chart that summarizes some of these ideas.

Activities	Inquiry
Activities have predetermined outcomes.	Inquiry fosters unanticipated outcomes.
Instructions are clear and convergent.	Instructions are open to several interpretations.
The teacher limits what materials are needed.	Children help to decide what materials are needed.
The teacher decides how to organize and display the data.	Children help to decide how to organize the information and keep records.
Integration is planned in advance for the teacher.	Integration arises from the children's questions.

This chart has been very helpful to me in thinking about how inquiry learning is different from other approaches to learning. David and I developed it after the pumpkin investigation that is described in Chapter 2. This chart has helped me rethink my role in the classroom community. It has made me more aware of encouraging children to solve their own problems.

One idea that I have come to value is to look for the unexpected. When children are given some ownership for posing their own questions, they set interesting challenges for themselves. I have found that if I really listen closely to what kids are saying, I will find some unexpected investigations to pursue. For instance, in this book some unexpected questions that arose were How many seeds are contained in the largest pumpkin ever grown? and How might the sides of a rectangle reflect a 3:1 ratio with the perimeter? I have learned that if I expect the unexpected, I'll find it. If I don't, I won't.

Another key idea in inquiry learning is to provide invitations that are open-ended. When investigations are open-ended, children can make sense of them in their own way. In this book you'll find some open-ended invitations, such as: What relationships can I find in this data about pumpkins? How can I define a circle? How can I make these shapes rigid? How can I figure out a way to compare the areas of these two shapes?

I have also come to see the value in letting children decide what materials they need. I realized that I often did too much for kids. An important aspect of the problem-solving process is deciding what materials are necessary. Sometimes I offer a range of materials to use, but the children are the ones who ultimately choose what to do. You'll find examples of this decision making in the book. For instance: What materials do I need to test the strength of my structure? What can I use to calculate the volume of a pumpkin? How can I determine the area of this shape? What measuring tool is best for measuring the length of the hallway?

The last idea that I would emphasize is to challenge children to organize and display data in their own way. I don't believe in those ready-made "graphic organizers" because they rob kids of rich learning opportunities. If we respect kids as sense makers, then we must give them the opportunity to organize and represent that data themselves. Later chapters offer examples of this idea, such as, How can I organize the pumpkin data to reveal a pattern? How can I keep track of the data about triangles to show a relationship? How can I draw an accurate picture of the Fort McHenry flag so my classmates understand how large it really was?

These ideas are important aspects of an inquiry classroom. If I encourage these ideas, I also help to build important mathematical attitudes and dispositions, such as initiative, confidence, resourcefulness, and risk taking. I feel that in a supportive mathematical community kids learn not only mathematical content and ideas, but also attitudes about themselves as learners. How they feel about themselves as problem solvers is a very important goal for me.

These ideas about inquiry learning are the ones that frame this book. Each chapter describes important facets of mathematical thinking and inquiring, such as posing one's own questions, keeping records of one's problem-solving efforts, extending initial problems into new mathematical territory, creating one's own tools, and uncovering patterns and relationships. In Chapter 6 I describe my rationale for a math workshop that I developed and how I fit it into my already busy schedule.

We decided to end the book with the children's reflections because they speak so eloquently about what it means to think mathematically. But we know that this thinking can happen only in a supportive mathematical community. So throughout the chapters, I have mentioned specific strategies I used to build this community. Enjoy this window into my classroom. I certainly don't know all the answers. I am still learning, like any inquirer. But I hope my story will give you a few insights into your own teaching, and together we'll improve the lives of all our students.

2 Mathematicians Keep Records and Pose Their Own Problems

Mathematicians enjoy posing problems and then finding ways to solve them. They also keep records of their findings so that they can share them with their collaborative community. In this chapter we describe a familiar experience with a pumpkin as a context for encouraging children to ask questions. We show children examining some measurements about pumpkins and then devising a question related to this data. In some cases the children actually extend their first investigation by posing an additional problem to pursue. This art of extending a math problem is discussed in more depth in Chapter 3. However, the beginnings of this problem posing began with the pumpkin experience, so it is important to understand how it first developed.

Robin had investigated using pumpkins with students in previous years. She had children estimate, weigh, and measure several pumpkins and then complete a guide sheet to tabulate the data for each pumpkin. She then recorded all the data on a large chart as a summary. The class celebrated the end of the activity by eating roasted pumpkin seeds together. As she thought back on the experience, she realized she had too narrowly defined the experience for the children by telling them what they were expected to investigate, how they were supposed to measure, and how they were supposed to organize their data. Each group of children always gathered the same kind of data and looked at it in the same way. She had always enjoyed the experience, as did the children, but this year she wanted the children to develop a sense of ownership for the project by encouraging them to create some of their own questions to investigate.

We felt the inquiry conditions (outlined in the introduction) would encourage diverse of responses from the children in terms of the questions they would ask, the relationships they might highlight, and the manner in which they would keep records of the process. It is this diversity that we felt would bring out individual voices, encourage a risk-taking stance, and generate alternative ways to investigate a set of data.

As we discussed these ideas further, Robin made the connection to the writer's workshop that she had been conducting in her room for several years. During this time children could choose their own writing topic, share their work with peers, and revise it along the way. Robin saw how this experience empowered her students as competent and confident writers in several ways. The children relished the control they had in choosing their topic. They would often try out different writing strategies that they discussed in class, such as creating an enticing lead sentence or creating an appropriate metaphor, because they knew their community of peers would support them. They also knew that they were the ones who always retained control of their writing. Robin wanted to develop this same kind of feeling in mathematics: confidence in one's ability to do mathematics and a willingness to engage in rigorous mathematical experiences. She felt that giving children the opportunity to ask their own questions was a clear parallel to her writer's workshop format, and she was eager to see how the children would respond.

The Investigation Begins

In order to give a general overview of the activity described in this chapter, we have included an outline, Lesson Plan and Intended Outcomes, that summarizes key outcomes for content and process. In this way readers can get a sense of the whole investigation, and therefore better appreciate the details of the story that follow. The content outcomes are tied directly to the district goals for fifth-grade mathematics. We have used this outline in the next two chapters as well so that readers have a clear picture what our goals are and how we intend to reach them.

We often used *Counting on Frank* as a springboard for generating some mathematical extensions. For instance, at the beginning of this investigation, we asked the students, "What would Frank's owner ask about pumpkins?" We used the story as a mathematical lens for viewing the pumpkins. The children's responses incorporated a variety of concepts and included such questions as:

1. What is the distance around a pumpkin? (length/circumference)
2. How small can a pumpkin get? (size)
3. How many baby pumpkins can fill a cabinet? (volume)
4. How many little pumpkins fit in each big pumpkin? (ratio and volume)
5. How long does it take for a pumpkin to grow? (time)
6. How much does a pumpkin weigh without the insides? (weight)
7. How many pumpkin lines can a pumpkin have around itself? (number and circumference)
8. How many seeds are in a pumpkin? (number)

We posted these questions on the wall underneath a drawing of Frank and his owner for reference during our investigations.

Next Robin gave a pumpkin to groups of four children and asked them to think about what basic mathematical information they wanted to gather about

Lesson Plan and Intended Outcomes

Lesson Plan	Intended Outcomes—Process	Intended Outcomes—Product
Children brainstorm different ways they could measure a pumpkin. (20 minutes)	Children view math as a way of looking at the world.	Children use measuring tools appropriately to calculate weight and circumference.
Children examine the data and devise a question to pursue. (15 minutes)	Children see themselves as initiators of math investigations.	Children find patterns and relationships in a given set of data.
Encourage a variety of investigations. (40 minutes)	Children see the relevance of math by using concepts in meaningful contexts.	Children use concepts of average, proportionality, volume, weight, and circumference.
Children share results with their classmates and reflect on the experience. (20 minutes)	Children view each other as valuable resources for understanding, representing, and communicating math content.	Children see how many different patterns and relationships can emerge from one set of data.

Class Pumpkin Chart

Pumpkin Number	Weight (pounds)	Circumference (inches)	No. of Vertical Lines	No. of Seeds
1	15	35	41	587
2	13½	34	22	696
3	15	36	34	466
4	13	36	21	529
5	13	33½	20	295
6	8½	31½	19	447

each of the pumpkins. Given the questions that they had just raised, the class decided upon the following essential information: the weight of each pumpkin, number of seeds, circumference, and number of vertical lines. Each group gathered the necessary data and Robin compiled it on a chart that the children used for further investigations.

In past years, the chart was the final product. However, now we wanted the children to use the data to pose their own questions.

Generating and Pursuing New Questions

We asked the children to think about the data they had gathered about pumpkins as well as the questions that Frank's owner might have asked about pumpkins, and to ask a question that was interesting for them to pursue. We told them they were not bound by the list of questions they had created earlier. The children formed questions that were quite varied and encompassed numerous mathematical concepts.

Melissa, Lindsay, and Tennille were interested in answering the question, "What is the biggest pumpkin in the world?" They began their exploration by checking a favorite reference book, *The Guinness Book of World Records* (Cunningham 1992). The girls found out that the biggest pumpkin on record was 816 pounds. When they shared this information with David, thinking their work was "done," David responded, "Now that you found this out, what are you wondering about?" We were trying to demonstrate to the children that investigations are never "finished." Answers are not final resting places, but only temporary stopping places for catching one's breath; they provide new information on which to inquire even further.

This attitude helps to foster one of the most important conditions of inquiry—developing an environment that nurtures the generation of knowledge. David's response was meant to show the students that the more they know, the more questions they can ask. The girls thought for a few seconds and then Lindsay responded, "Well, I wonder how many seeds there would be in a pumpkin that large!" The other girls agreed that this "wonder" would be an interesting one to pursue. When David asked, "How could you figure that out?" the girls were not quite sure how to proceed. Together David and the girls looked back at the class data and found that the largest pumpkin weighed 15 pounds and had an average of 525 seeds (there were two 15-pound pumpkins and the girls figured the average). Although David was thinking to himself that an effective strategy might be to divide 816 by 15 to determine the number of 15-pound pumpkins, and then multiply that answer by 525 to find the total number of seeds, the girls had a different strategy. Lindsay suggested an adding-on strategy to solve the problem: "If we had two pumpkins, that would be 30 pounds, and then we could just keep on adding till we got to 816." However, they found it was quicker to double the numbers (Figure 2–1), and continued to do so until they reached 960 pounds. Realizing that this final figure was too high, they subtracted 100 and then four sets of ten to get a closer total of 820 pounds. They knew they also had to adjust the total number of seeds and so subtracted 140 from 33,600. This last calculation was not quite accurate, since they did not take into account the proportion of 825 seeds per 15 pounds. We discussed the proportionality with the girls later on. Robin was particularly struck with the mathematics the girls used in their investigation. They used the concept of a ratio and the strategy of doubling to solve their problem. Their actions were in sharp contrast to previous years when children gathered and reported the same kind of results. Now that the children had ownership for the question, they were able to demonstrate a range of mathematical insights.

In a later conversation, some of their classmates used the group data chart to challenge the girls' findings by pointing out that there seemed to be no relationship between the number of seeds and the weight of the pumpkin. In fact, Brandon looked at that relationship for one of his investigations and concluded, "There appears to be no effect on the weight because of the seeds" (Figure 2–2). Using Brandon's study as evidence, some of the children argued that the final calculation for the total number of seeds in the 816-pound pumpkin might not be accurate. The girls simply responded, "We know that! But *if* it was related this is what it would be." In hindsight we realized that the girls could have argued that their method capitalized on one of the benefits of an average (mean): It evens out extremes, since the number of seeds contained in the two 15-pound pumpkins varied widely (587 and 466). Nevertheless, their work certainly portrayed them as mathematicians in their own right: They posed their own question, devised an appropriate solution strategy, kept careful records of the process, and defended their work in front of their peers.

In contrast to this investigation about the largest pumpkin, Amanda wanted to explore how small a pumpkin could be. She wrote, "I explored how small can a pumpkin get. A pumpkin can get as small as a baby's ear. I know that because my grandpa grows pumpkins and he told me." She then used this reference to an ear to help her calculate how many little pumpkins would fit into a desk.

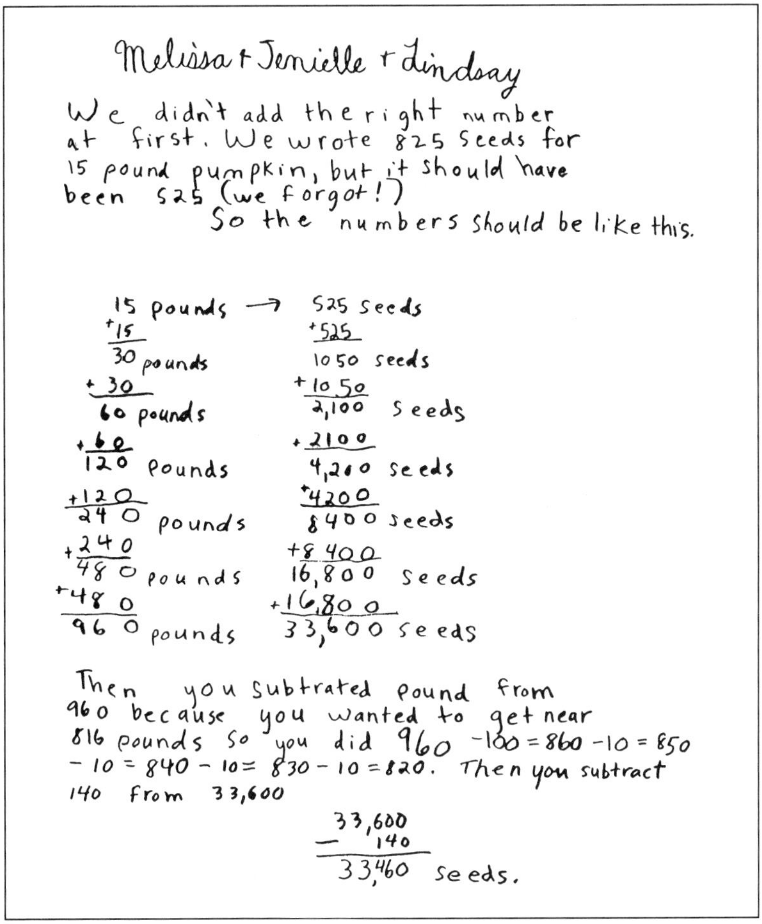

> Melissa + Jenielle + Lindsay
>
> We didn't add the right number at first. We wrote 825 seeds for 15 pound pumpkin, but it should have been 525 (we forgot!)
>   So the numbers should be like this.
>
> ```
> 15 pounds  →    525 seeds
> +15             +525
> ─────           ─────
> 30 pounds       1050 seeds
> +30             +1050
> ─────           ─────
> 60 pounds       2,100 seeds
> +60             +2100
> ─────           ─────
> 120 pounds      4,200 seeds
> +120            +4200
> ─────           ─────
> 240 pounds      8400 seeds
> +240            +8400
> ─────           ─────
> 480 pounds      16,800 seeds
> +480            +16,800
> ─────           ─────
> 960 pounds      33,600 seeds
> ```
>
> Then you subtrated pound from 960 because you wanted to get near 816 pounds so you did 960 -100 = 860 -10 = 850 -10 = 840 -10 = 830 -10 = 820. Then you subtract 140 from 33,600
>
> ```
>   33,600
> -    140
> ───────
>   33,460 seeds.
> ```

Figure 2–1

Choice allowed Amanda to make a personal connection to pumpkins and to explore the concept of volume at the same time.

Ruth initiated a slightly different investigation when she wondered, "Is the circumference the same as the distance around the other way?" We suspected that Ruth's instructional history told her that the circumference of a sphere, as illustrated in a typical textbook, was the distance *horizontally* around a sphere. She wondered if the distance vertically around a sphere (in this case, a pumpkin) was the same as the distance horizontally around a sphere (Figure 2–3). Her question was also pushing the definition of circumference: Does it count if it is used vertically? Does the term *circumference* apply only to spheres, or can it be applied to other shapes? (*The Oxford English Dictionary* defines a circumference as "an enclosing boundary, especially of a circle or other figure enclosed

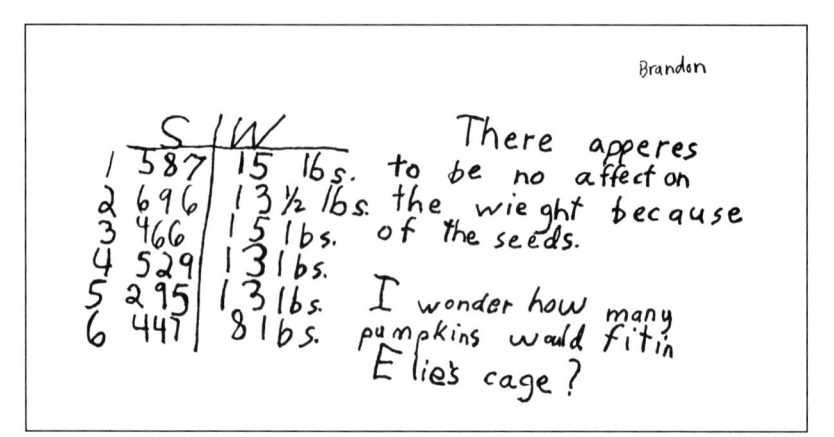

Mathematicians Keep Records and Pose Their Own Problems

Brandon

S	W
1 587	15 lbs.
2 696	13½ lbs.
3 466	15 lbs.
4 529	13 lbs.
5 295	13 lbs.
6 447	8 lbs.

There apperes to be no affect on the wieght because of the seeds.

I wonder how many pumpkins would fit in Elie's cage?

Figure 2–2

I wonder if the circumference is almost the same answer as from the top of the pumpkin to the bottom then back to the top.

My answer is 3 feet each it was the same. I used group fives pumpkin picture →

3 feet
3 feet
string
All the way around

I did #2's pumpkin & it was 3'5" & 3'5" the same again. I did pumkin number 6 next & around it was 2'9" and up was 2'9" same again Pumpkin 4 around was 3'7" and 3'5" Pumpkin 4 was fatter than the rest.

Figure 2–3

by a curve.") In hindsight we felt that we could have explored this definition more with her. However, her investigation highlighted for us the potential for children to create their own definitions for mathematical terms. This issue is described more fully in Chapter 3.

She found that the distance from "the top of the pumpkin to the bottom then back to the top" was the same on all the pumpkins except for pumpkin #4. She made a drawing of one of the pumpkins so she could show the horizontal and vertical measurements. Her investigation helped show the relationship between circumference and shape. Ruth was also demonstrating to the class that drawing was a valuable way to record one's mathematical thinking.

Melissa nicely demonstrated how posing one question can lead to the generation of others, an important condition of inquiry learning. Her first investigation involved the concept of average. She wrote in her journal, "Today I was exploring the question, 'How many vertical lines were on the average large pumpkin?' I added up all of our six pumpkins' vertical lines, then divided by the six since there were six pumpkins. I got an average of 26, but that was only for six pumpkins. I wonder what it would be if you used like 50 pumpkins to get your average." Melissa viewed her answer as tentative as she posed another problem for herself. She used the word "wonder," which the class adopted, to extend the problem even further. Although she obviously could not gather data on fifty pumpkins, the important point was that she modified one of the variables of her problem—the number of pumpkins—to pose another problem. She was displaying important mathematical attitudes by challenging the data and by questioning whether the size of the sample was sufficient. In this way new information does not lie dormant but provides the basis for further hypothesizing. This was part of the spirit of an inquiry classroom that we were trying to foster.

Posing Questions About Relationships

Brandon posed a question about the relationship between the height and weight of the pumpkins. He began his investigation by recording the weights of the pumpkins from the chart and then measuring the heights of the pumpkins. As he began to look at both columns of his data (Figure 2–4), he noticed a pattern: "There are 1½ differences between weight and height. I think it's a pattern." The measurements for four out of the six pumpkins displayed this pattern. Unfortunately, in the midst of this classroom investigation, the other two pumpkins had to be thrown away because they had deteriorated so badly (pumpkins in a warm classroom do not last long!). However, these missing two pumpkins did not bother Brandon. He had already established a pattern of "1½ differences"; since he already had the weight of the two missing pumpkins from the class chart, he was able to predict the height of these pumpkins (by subtracting 1½). However, to differentiate between his actual and predicted measurements, he wrote "actual" and "don't know" beside each of his results. Thus, Brandon pursued a relationship that was intriguing for him and engaged in the work of real mathematicians. He confronted the problem of missing data, a common problem among statisticians. He extrapolated

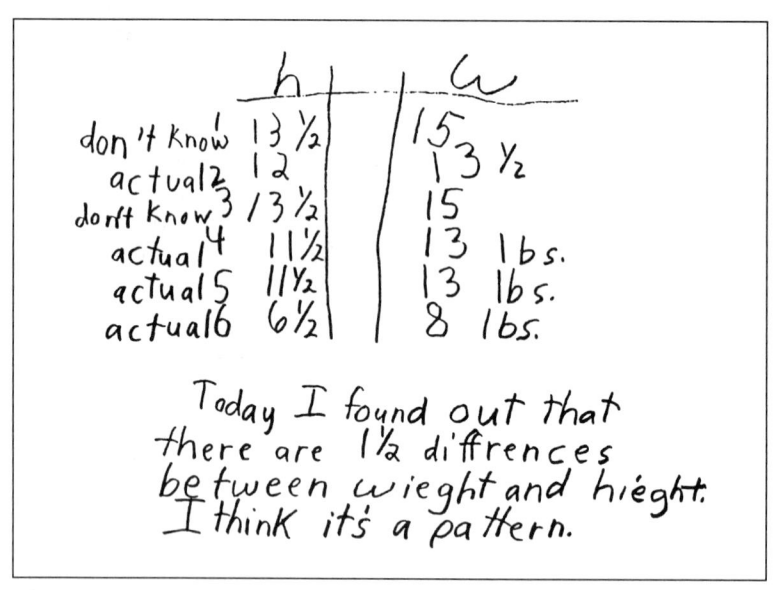

> h | w
> don't know¹ 13½ | 15
> actual² 12 | 13½
> don't know³ 13½ | 15
> actual⁴ 11½ | 13 lbs.
> actual⁵ 11½ | 13 lbs.
> actual⁶ 6½ | 8 lbs.
>
> Today I found out that there are 1½ diffrences between wieght and hieght. I think it's a pattern.

Figure 2–4

(inferred) the missing data by identifying a pattern, and then reclassified the data to show this refinement of his results.

Anna became intrigued not only with the weight of pumpkins but also with her estimates about those weights. She used a line graph (Figure 2–5) to show that her estimates were usually higher than the actual weight; she was the only one in the class who was interested in this contrast and invented an interesting way to depict the difference. Thus, Anna and Brandon demonstrated additional ways that mathematicians keep records, that is, through charts and graphs.

Posing Questions About Volume

Several students were interested in questions that dealt with volume. However, some of their journal entries revealed a misunderstanding of what volume is and how it ought to be calculated. Jenny asked, "How many seeds would it take to fill up a big pumpkin?" (Figure 2–6). Jenny took the distance (twenty-four inches) around the base of her pumpkin (which is where most of the seeds were located) and multiplied it by the number of seeds (295) in her pumpkin. It made sense to her that the girth would be an important measure to consider in her calculations. It also made sense to multiply in order to add these several layers of seeds. However, she failed to consider the height as a key factor in determining the volume.

LaToya also posed a question related to volume: "I wonder how many little pumpkins can fill a big pumpkin? Well, first I need to measure. If your big pumpkin's weight is 30 lbs. and a little pumpkin's weight is 8 lbs., then 3 pumpkins and one 6 lb. pumpkin could fit." She then drew a picture to convey the information in another way (Figure 2–7). LaToya demonstrated another mis-

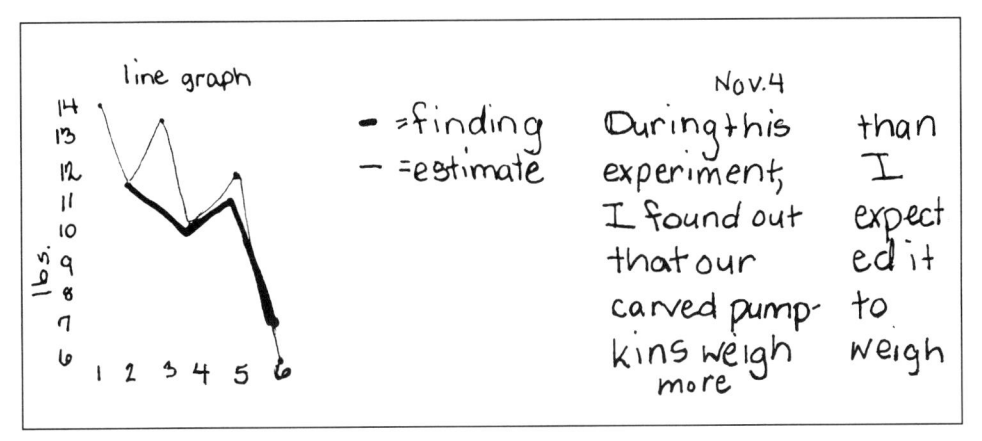

Figure 2–5

understanding about volume by considering weight and volume as synonymous; she reasoned that things that weighed the same ought to have the same volume.

Melissa posed a question about volume but tested it in a more concrete way. She wrote: "How many little pumpkins will fit in a big pumpkin?" Melissa chose

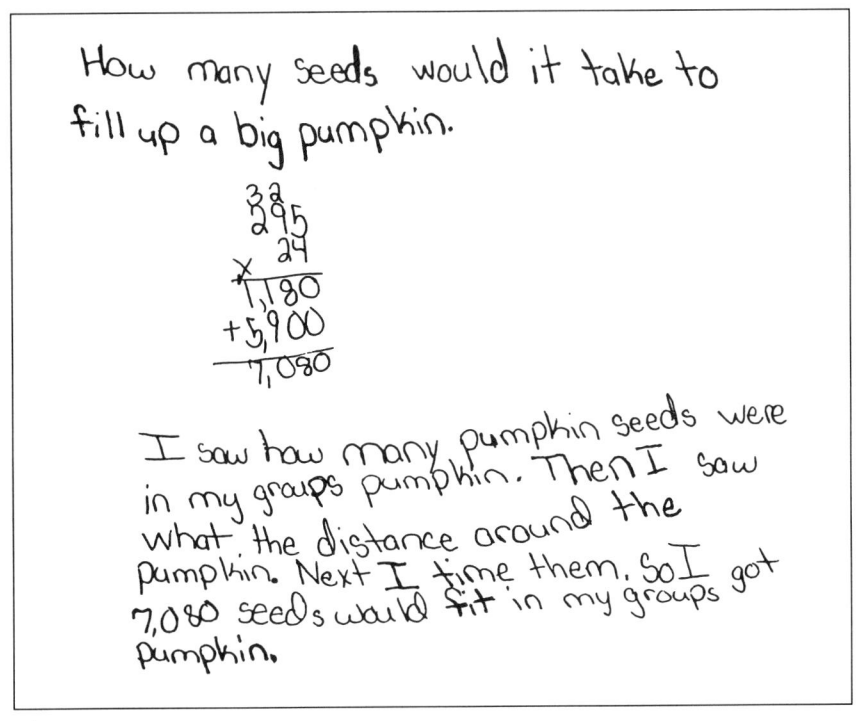

Figure 2–6

> I wonder how many little pumpkins can full a big pumpkins? Well first I need to measure. If your big pumpkins weight 30 and a little pumpkins weigh 8 than 3 pumpkins and one 6 weight pumpkin could fit.
>
> But it would be full (…maybe?)
>
> What I did today? Well what Me and Jenny did today was exciting it take a lot of thinking. On the back you see what we did. I discover that it takes a lot of thinking to do math. I wonder who made the measuring tape because it is easier to work with measuring tape than a ruler.
>
> LaToya

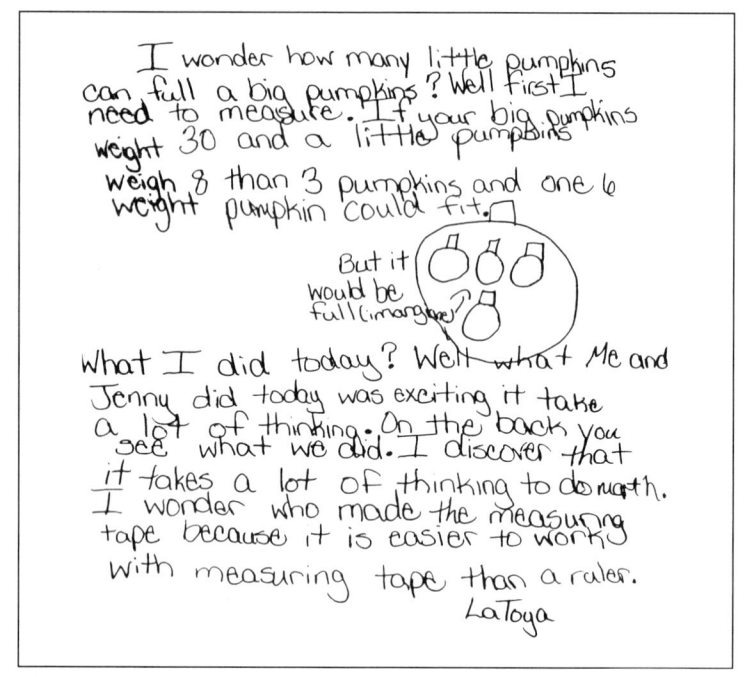

Figure 2–7

to crumple up sheets of paper to the size that she thought a small pumpkin would be. She then stuffed the paper pumpkins inside the larger pumpkin to actually see the number of little pumpkins that would fit inside a large pumpkin. Melissa was demonstrating that making models is an important strategy for mathematicians to use. When the students shared their various questions and the results of their explorations, Melissa, Jenny, and LaToya took note of the ways in which they chose to investigate the same question.

As we think back on the experience, we realized we could have been more explicit about how Melissa's strategy demonstrated the meaning of volume. At the same time we could have recognized the efforts of the other two girls in incorporating important ideas about volume in their investigations. Jenny used the base of the pumpkin, and LaToya saw the importance of filling up the space inside the pumpkin. We might have tested these ideas further. For instance, we might have crumpled up different weights of paper to show how weight is not a factor in determining volume. Or we might have calculated the number of seeds by multiplying the number that covered the base by the height (using the height of the seed base to estimate the number of height units for multiplying). Although we did not discuss in enough detail these different strategies for calculating volume, we did come to realize that children have various ideas about volume, and we needed to spend more time discussing this concept in the future. We were coming to see that this investigation gave us valuable assessment information.

Children had some beginning notions about volume but needed more concrete experiences to understand the concept of measuring three-dimensional objects.

Reflecting on the Process

After they completed their investigations with pumpkins, we had a lengthy sharing time so everyone could explain their findings to the rest of the class. Then we had the children reflect on the importance of having these sharing sessions as well as comment on other wonders they might still be entertaining. We believe that reflection about the process is an essential condition of inquiry. It gives children a time to think back on the entire experience: the setting of questions, the investigations themselves, and the sharing of results.

Tanya's comment underscored the generative nature of classroom discussions: "Having us share makes me think more about how other people think and makes you want to explore more by my opinion." Melissa B. also validated the importance of group discussions when she commented, "I gained more ways to figure questions out by listening to people." Several students, such as Horace, remarked on the way Anna displayed her data: "I like the line graph Anna did. I think that it is interesting." Brett was intrigued with Brandon's results and wrote: "I also thought Brandon had a neat pattern with what he found out." Brandon himself reflected on his experience with volume. He had calculated the number of pumpkins that would fit in Ellie's (the class rabbit) cage, and remarked later that it was difficult to determine exactly how many pumpkins would fit because there were all these spaces in between. He wrote in his journal, "I found another question: If pumpkins were square, how many would fit in Ellie's cage? It would be easier to measure." He was developing an understanding of why certain shapes are used for determining volume. Last, Nigel commented on the value of posing his own questions (or "wonders"): "I think 'I wonder' makes you try to explore more. You also try to do sort of like research. I wonder if you took a cube about this size." He drew the base of a cube in his journal and posed the following questions: "How many quarts would fit into this? If I got 80 quarts of the same size how many cups would fit into this? Gee, maybe you should divide." Nigel enjoyed the challenge of posing his own questions because it encouraged him to "explore more." Although he did not pursue the answer to his cube question, he was certainly demonstrating the kind of inquiry spirit that we were trying to nurture in the classroom.

What We Learned About the Process of Inquiry

These investigations with pumpkins helped illuminate important features of inquiry learning. Robin noticed that students' questions were quite varied and challenged them as learners. She was struck with how much more the children were capable of doing in mathematics as she compared the experience with the more structured data-gathering activity that she had conducted in the past. She also observed that open-ended experiences placed us teachers in the role of learners from the very beginning. It was clear to the students that we did not immediately know the answers to the questions they were posing. When children sense that teacher and student share ownership of a collaborative venture, they are more willing to take some risks and share their thinking with others. Our role as learners supported them in being more inquisitive learners.

We also learned that keeping instructions fairly open-ended probably encouraged children to pursue a wide range of problems, particularly aspects of the data that seemed surprising to them, such as, "Shouldn't pumpkins that weigh more have more seeds?" and "Shouldn't the circumference of a pumpkin just be measured horizontally and not vertically?" We learned that if children are in charge of formulating their own investigation, then they also need to be in charge of gathering the appropriate materials to solve that problem. Plenty of materials were available: scales, measuring tapes, string, calculators, and so forth. However, they needed to decide which tools they needed rather than having the required materials listed for them in advance. From an inquiry perspective, children also need to display their findings in many ways; we noticed that children used charts, line graphs, sketches, three-dimensional drawings, narratives, and so on. We also saw that as children explored a variety of patterns and relationships, they naturally integrated many mathematical concepts, such as average, volume, weight, quantity, equivalence, and length.

Robin saw this experience with pumpkins as an important demonstration of what it means to think mathematically. She saw her students investigating and exploring just as mathematicians do, moving beyond the boundaries of a prescribed activity. David was struck by the language that the children used in their journals to describe their mathematical endeavors—words such as *explored, investigated, discovered, wondered*. These were the very words that we, as teachers, had used from the beginning of the year to describe any mathematical work we did together. Now the children had accessed this language and made it their own. We were realizing that the language we used in the classroom served to identify us as a unique social and intellectual community and helped us frame how we saw and thought about the world.

Going Beyond the Experience

As we looked back on this investigation with pumpkins, we thought about important lessons we learned along the way. These lessons included the following activities:

1. Start the year with a book that demonstrates what it means to think mathematically. We chose *Counting on Frank* (Clement 1991). Other interesting titles that foster a mathematical view of the world are *How Much Is a Million?* (Schwartz 1985) and *Math Curse* (Scieszka 1995).

2. Invite students to list "wonders" they have after exploring a particular mathematical topic. Use these wonders as possible invitations for

children to investigate further. Other questions to pose include: What do you find interesting about what you discovered? What are you still curious about? (Schillereff 2001).

3. Invite children to collect measurements and statistics about topics that interest them. We used pumpkins. Other children might use rocks (weight, color, size, etc.), weather (temperature, cloud cover, precipitation), or parking lots (number of cars, make, year, and style). Have students organize this data in their own way. Encourage them to interpret the data and pose "wonders" they have about the information.

4. After a class discussion ask children to record in their math journal what they found interesting about the conversation and why. Share these reflections so that children recognize the benefits of learning in a collaborative community.

5. During class discussions, highlight the different ways that children represent their thinking. Make an ongoing wall chart of different strategies for representing ideas, such as charts and tables, graphs, or sketches. Discuss the potentials and limitations of each form of representation.

3 Mathematicians Are Skeptics Who Go Beyond the Data

An important attitude of mathematicians is to be skeptical. They question results, challenge assumptions, and wonder if conclusions are valid. Skepticism is a sign of good mathematical health because it means that learners are thinking in a critical way. However, this skepticism can flourish only in an inquiry community that encourages risk taking, seeks out questions from all children, and values doubt as a way to generate further understanding. In this chapter you will hear Robert and other children demonstrate this skeptical attitude during an investigation of circles. He wondered whether the ratio of circumference to diameter (3:1) was really true for all circles. His skepticism helped the community grow by launching them into a more concrete exploration of this relationship.

Mathematicians also go beyond the data (Davis 1964). There were several examples of this kind of thinking in Chapter 2. For instance, Melissa found the average number of vertical lines on six pumpkins, and then wondered how her results might be different if she measured fifty pumpkins. We challenged the three girls who found the largest pumpkin to go beyond the data. They decided to figure out the number of seeds in a pumpkin that large (816 pounds). In both examples the children used their initial answer as a basis for posing additional wonders. In this chapter you will hear more about this process of extending investigations and why it reflects the true nature of mathematical thinking and inquiry. We describe in this chapter how Jason sets a new mathematical direction for the class by wondering if the ratio of circumference to diameter (3:1) for circles would be true with other shapes. For instance, is there a 3:1 ratio between the perimeter of a square and its diagonal? Or the perimeter of a triangle and its height? His hypothesis clearly went beyond the present investigation of circles and demonstrated the strategy of problem posing (Brown and Walter 1990) in which learners modify the attributes of a given problem (circles) to pose further problems (ratios with other shapes).

Stephen Brown and Marion Walter, well-known mathematics educators who have been advocating the benefits of this strategy for decades, strongly believe that this playful attitude toward problem variables is an essential part of an inquiring mind. They claim the more opportunities that learners have to change a given problem (or rule, algorithm, design, etc.), the better they will understand it. This attitude is in sharp contrast to the prevalent (although changing) view of instruction in which mathematics is seen as a world of fixed rules and tightly held assumptions that are never questioned or modified in any way; this perspective assumes that changing things merely confuses learners and "takes away" precious time from the task at hand. However, as Brown and Walter discuss the benefits of problem posing, we felt there was a strong parallel between those advantages and the conditions of inquiry that we had embraced as teachers:

1. Problem posing generates new understandings by enabling learners to see common things in uncommon ways. Jason's question caused all of us, including teachers, to view regular and irregular shapes in a new way as we examined closely the relationship between perimeter and height/length. His wonder supported the voices of all learners as different children experimented with a variety of shapes and reported their results to the class.

2. Problem posing helps demonstrate that being vulnerable and taking a risk makes us grow as a mathematical community. No one was sure what mathematical relationships we would discover as we examined other shapes. Part of being a mathematical inquirer is traveling paths that are not well marked.

3. Problem posing encourages reflection about the process. As children tested new shapes, they reflected on what they had learned about circles, enabling them to make comparisons and predictions about their new findings.

4. Problem posing helps build a sense of community by fostering a spirit of adventure and intellectual excitement. Children eagerly sought to test Jason's hypothesis, partly because they had conducted the first investigation together and had a vested interest in wanting to go further. His question also developed a sense of community because it demonstrated that teacher and students were coequals in such a collaborative venture. Jason's hypothesis pushed us teachers to think anew about the relationship between perimeter and the height/length of various shapes. The children knew we were learning along with them, and this attitude contributed to the collaborative nature of our investigation.

The Investigation Begins

The following lesson plan for this investigation highlights key mathematical attitudes and strategies (process) as well as curricular content for the fifth grade (product).

Our assessment of the children's work with pumpkins prompted us to begin an exploration of circles. This decision was based on several observations. First,

Lesson Plan and Intended Outcomes

Lesson Plan	Intended Outcomes—Process	Intended Outcomes—Product
Children measure the circumference and diameter of various objects. (40 minutes)	Children share a wide range of objects; they decide for themselves how to format their results.	Children identify diameter and circumference of circles; they systematically collect and organize data.
Children analyze the data for patterns. (20 minutes)	Children view the making of patterns as the work of mathematicians.	Children determine the relationship between the diameter and circumference (ratio).
Conduct a class discussion of findings. (20 minutes)	Children use their own language to describe the relationship; they question the results.	Children use data to construct generalizations; they investigate similarity of all circles.
Children reflect on the investigation. (20 minutes)	Children pose their own questions; they use the findings of one investigation as a catalyst for posing a new exploration.	Children extend this generalization about circles to other polygons; they discuss relationships of sides of rectangles, squares, and triangles.
Challenge children to write their own definition of a circle. (20 minutes)	Children view math definitions as human inventions, based upon agreed-upon attributes.	Children classify polygons using many different attributes.

we noticed that the children used the distance around (circumference) as one of their measurements of the pumpkins. Second, we noticed that many of the children were unaccustomed to measuring around objects; like most children in school, their only experiences with measuring had involved a ruler. (We did in fact witness a few students trying to use their plastic rulers to measure around a pumpkin.) Based on these classroom observations we wanted to provide the children with another experience in which they could measure around circular objects. Third, we wanted them to address the district goal of understanding the meaning of π.

We asked the children to measure the circumference and diameter of various circular objects in the room and then analyze their results for any patterns. We distributed cloth measuring tapes and encouraged them to measure a wide range of objects, from a small jar lid to a large wastebasket. After this initial exploration we came together to discuss our observations.

Discussing Our Findings

The children made a personal list of their findings in their math journals; we later recorded some of their results on the board. Brandon's journal entry (Figure 3–1) shows some of the objects he measured, such as various buckets, lids, and containers, as well as his conclusion: "I think when you do this you're just adding the diameter 3 times." However, Brandon's note in the side margin reflects his surprise at the results: "I wonder how a number can triple and be the same." He was amazed that this 3:1 ratio, which he nicely described as a "tripling" phenomenon, could remain the same even though the class had measured a wide range of objects. Other children offered still further observations. Anna remarked, "The

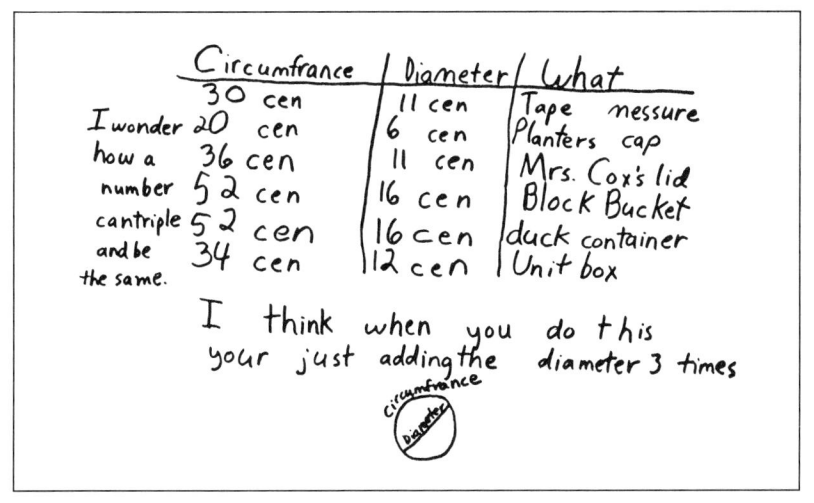

Figure 3–1

circumference is always higher than the diameter." Jason described the relationship in this way: "Three times the number. You triple it. Usually the circumference and diameter is related. It is somewhere near triple the amount of the diameter." He proved his idea by multiplying several diameters by 3, such as 70 mm × 3 mm = 210 mm and 40 mm × 3 mm = 120 mm, to show that the answer was quite close to the circumference that was actually measured. Ruth noticed that the dimensions of the round light that she measured reflected this 3:1 ratio exactly. Robert wanted to check some of his answers by doing just the reverse; he divided one of his circumference measurements by 3, such as 360/3 = 120, to see if his answer of 120 was close to the measurement of his diameter (which he had measured to be 112). Thus, the children wanted to test out this ratio and found some interesting ways to do it.

The conversation continued as we asked, "Why does this ratio of 3:1 seem to be true for all circles, no matter how big or small they are?" Jason, who seemed particularly intrigued by this relationship, responded: "A circle is a circle. It might be bigger or smaller but they are all the same. How come it takes three diameters to make a circle? Maybe width times length, or width times circumference, equals something like that. The larger the circle gets the larger the diameter gets."

Jason's comments demonstrated his understanding that ratios are proportionate, noting that the diameter gets larger (proportionately) as the circle gets larger. His statement that "A circle is a circle" also highlights the idea that all circles are similar, that is, they may be different sizes but they are all proportionate. Although Jason did not use the technical terms *ratio*, *proportion*, and *similarity*, he certainly described them quite well in his own way. We did introduce these terms to the children later on in the investigation, but we felt it was important that they continue to use their own language to describe these mathematical ideas. In this way we could better evaluate their understanding of these concepts.

Like several of his classmates, Nigel still voiced his uncertainty about the results because he felt the diameter ought to be half the length of the circumference. It was surprising to him that it took three diameters to go around a circle because he was convinced it ought to be only two. He was struggling to come to grips with what "appears" versus what the data revealed. Brandon tried to convince him that a diameter was a straight line, and half a circumference was a "stretched out" line. This discussion about the shortest distance between two points did not get resolved at this time; others raised the issue later on, as the children became involved in further investigations. It was important to nurture this skepticism because it not only allowed others to voice this concern but also encouraged Brandon to explain this anomaly to his peers.

Jason raised another question about this relationship between circumference and diameter. Although he had been quite confident earlier about his results on ratio, he now wanted to share an observation that disturbed him. His willingness to voice this doubt was a healthy sign of risk taking, leading to further understanding for himself and the class. He created a chart to explain his puzzlement to the class:

Diameter	Circumference
1	1 × 3 = 3
2	2 × 3 = 6
3	3 × 3 = 9
4	4 × 3 = 12

He knew that it was appropriate to keep tripling the diameter to get the circumference. However, when he looked at the circumferences of 3, 6, 9, and 12, he noticed that the second one (6) was double the first (3), and so he predicted that the circumferences ought to continue to double, that is, 3, 6, 12, 24. However, his results of 3, 6, 9, and 12 did not show this doubling and he wanted to know why. He created another chart to show this doubling and realized that in order for the circumference to double he had to double the diameter as well (in contrast to his first chart, where the diameter was only increasing by one each time).

Diameter	Circumference
1	1 × 3 = 3
2	2 × 3 = 6
4	4 × 3 = 12
8	8 × 3 = 24

His investigation was helping the class build a beginning understanding of ratios and how they work, that is, multiplication creates equivalent ratios. He was also demonstrating some of the attitudes and dispositions of mathematical thinkers: being intrigued with the unexpected, wondering why these results occurred, and devising a plan to understand the mathematics of the situation.

Skepticism Leads to Further Investigating

After the children shared their findings with each other we asked them to record in their journals what they had learned and what ideas they were still wondering about. Robert was one of several children who questioned the results (Figure 3–2), wondering "if it [the 3:1 ratio] works on all circles." Other students still wondered if perhaps two diameters could stretch around a circle, not three. We were a bit surprised at their skepticism. We felt that the numerical results they had obtained would have been sufficient proof. However, we were pleased that they were willing to share this skepticism, refusing to believe what did not make sense to them. Too often in mathematics classrooms children abandon their sense-making capabilities for rules and procedures that yield right answers but do not make sense. We wanted to be sure we continued to nurture this sense-making strategy. It was these lingering doubts that prompted us to recast the investigation in a more concrete way. We asked them to cut string the length of the diameter of each circle and then tape as many diameters as they could around the

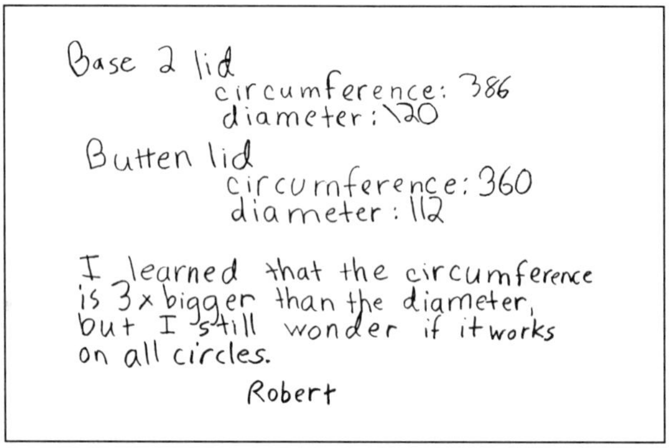

> Base 2 lid
>   circumference: 386
>   diameter: 120
>
> Butten lid
>   circumference: 360
>   diameter: 112
>
> I learned that the circumference is 3x bigger than the diameter, but I still wonder if it works on all circles.
>   Robert

Figure 3–2

circumference. The children were eager to try representing this ratio in a more physical, tactile way.

Horace was one of the first people to get started because he was particularly skeptical of the initial findings (Figure 3–3). He was so convinced that it should take only two diameters to go around a circle that he actually redid his first investigation because he could not quite believe the outcome. He did not even want to test another circle until he verified the results of his first measurement. We were pleased that Horace felt comfortable enough to say, "Can I do this again? I'm still not sure about this." He was demonstrating the healthy attitude of an inquirer, unwilling to accept an idea until it made sense to him and persisting in making a further test of his results. We have found that children will often willingly check and redo their work when there is a legitimate reason to do so. We wanted to support this skepticism because we felt it was an important aspect of our inquiring community.

Robin supported this skeptical attitude in several ways:

1. She posed questions that invited a skeptical stance. For example: Is this pattern/relationship always true, or does it occur in just certain cases? Is this something we can really believe? Do we have the evidence to support this claim?

2. She encouraged children to raise questions about issues from different perspectives, such as, How do Native Americans feel about the "discovery" of America? Looking at an event from multiple perspectives makes learners skeptical about accepting a single interpretation.

3. She posed extension questions—for instance, Now that we discovered this relationship, what are you wondering about? Robin wanted her children to realize that answers are not final resting places, but the seeds for new questions.

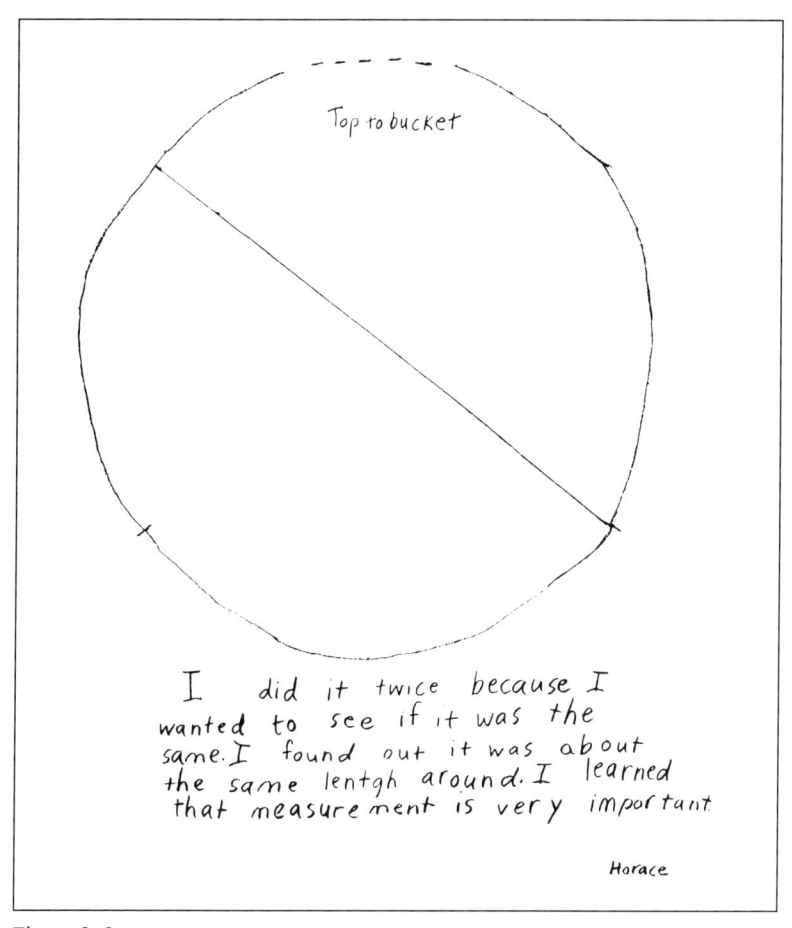

Figure 3–3

4. She encouraged her children to examine data in a critical way by asking, What questions does this survey not answer? Who would benefit from gathering the data in this way?

As the children continued to work we were again struck by how surprised many of them were that these results using string matched the numerical results of our first exploration. The children needed more opportunities to test this idea. Even when we did use string, several children, including Horace, redid several measurements on their own because they were still unconvinced of the results. We were glad that these children still questioned the findings because they were sharing their vulnerability as learners in the process. Voicing this kind of uncertainty builds an inquiring community. We also realized that if we had just asked them to memorize the formula for this relationship ($C = \pi \times d$), they would have only been parroting it back to us, rather than explaining it with a well-tested understanding.

Tennille, like several other children, discovered that this 3:1 ratio was only an approximation. As she stretched three lengths of a diameter around the circumference of a circle she noticed that there was always a portion of the circumference that was not covered. For instance, after measuring a circular mailbox tube and a marker can, she found it is "true that it takes three to go around the circle." She added, "I learned that it always leaves a space" (the .1417 in the conventional decimal representation of π, 3.1417). By looking at just the earlier numerical results, many of the children were not sure what that decimal portion represented; this more concrete experience helped them describe the remaining length in a more visual way. Ruth measured some different round objects (Figure 3–4) and found a relationship between the size of the gap and the size of the circle: "I noticed that in littler circles there's littler gaps and in bigger circles there's bigger gaps." Her focus on the remainder helped to demonstrate to the class the similarity of circles, that is, the size of the remainder is proportionate to the size of the circle. This second investigation with string enabled Ruth and others to highlight this new understanding.

Brent described this relationship in another way when he wrote: "I learned when the circle gets larger the line across the middle expands more. I also learned the circle is going to have some space still left." Lee wrote: "I learned about the

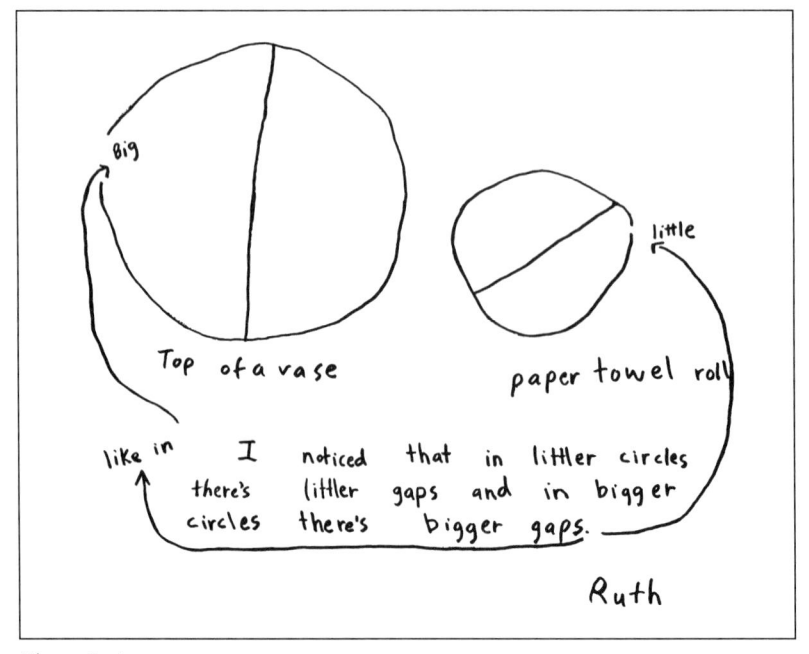

Figure 3–4

circles that the bigger the circle the more the string [is left uncovered]. The less the size, the less the string" [is left uncovered]. Using a variety of descriptive terms, such as *expands*, *less*, *more*, and *exact*, the children described this important mathematical relationship in their own way. We encouraged these diverse descriptions because they not only celebrated a range of individual voices but also highlighted the proportional relationship among all circles.

These examples illustrate Robin's goal that her students learn mathematics with understanding. They also highlight her belief that an inquiry perspective helps promote that understanding. Robin knew that asking questions, wondering why, and sharing unexpected results were ways that children could go beyond the surface-level knowledge of mathematics and gain a deeper understanding of the concepts. She encouraged her children to pose questions in a variety of ways:

1. She asked questions herself that focused on the process of sense making, such as, Why did it make sense for you to solve it in that way? Robin felt that if children were recognized as sense makers they would be more willing to ask questions when certain ideas or relationships did *not* make sense.

2. She publicly recognized children for asking questions: "Melissa, thank you for sharing that question. Your question has helped the class rethink their ideas about calculating area."

3. She posted charts of questions that the children generated in all subject areas, such as "wonders" about the ocean, the Civil War, or fractions.

4. She kept soliciting questions *throughout* an investigation, not just at the beginning. For instance, Robin regularly asked, How did the blocks help you understand division? What are you still wondering about?

5. She was a questioner herself, often contributing to class discussions as a fellow inquirer.

Mathematicians Go Beyond the Data

After the children used string to measure the diameter and circumference of circles, we thought the investigation had ended. We asked the children to record in their journals what they had learned as well as any further wonderings they still had. It was Jason's wonder (Figure 3–5) that set us on our new journey. He wondered if this same theory—a 3:1 ratio between distance around and distance across—was true for other shapes, such as squares, triangles, or even squiggly-looking irregular shapes. As he shared his wonder with the group, no one was quite sure how to answer his question, including us teachers. His theoretical wondering had opened a new area for exploration and we were all invited in as fellow investigators. We asked the children to test Jason's theory on a variety of shapes for homework (since Jason had raised this wonder at the end of the day).

Figure 3–5

His question helped us reflect on the conditions of inquiry that we were trying to foster in the classroom. We saw that asking open-ended questions encouraged the children to take risks, generate new insights, and build a sense of community. We were also learning that an important aspect of community is having children see their teachers being challenged intellectually. We were not sure what we might find if we explored other shapes, and the children read that uncertainty on our faces. We are convinced that unless we admit to children the limits of our own knowledge, and are willing to set out together on uncharted waters, then we will continually restrict the potential we have as a community of fellow inquirers.

Jason was the first to share his homework the next day. He created an amorphous shape (Figure 3–6) and found a ratio of 4:1, commenting that these results were not "normal," but "of course the shape you see above is not a geometric shape." Thus, he wondered if more regular geometric shapes might still possess this 3:1 ratio, arguing that his curvilinear shape might be an exception. He waited to hear what his other classmates had discovered.

A few children investigated squares. For instance, Melissa E. used both the diagonal and the length of the side to see if either one stretched around the perimeter of the square about three times. She wrote in her journal: "Today I found that on a square the diagonal line is always bigger than the straight up and down line. I am confused about whether or not when a square gets bigger the gap gets bigger or not. On a circle the gap gets bigger when the circle gets bigger but on a square I think the bigger the square is the more string you have left over." She found three diagonals could not fit around a square (they were too long) but three side lengths always left a gap (that is, the length of the fourth side) and wondered if this gap would get bigger as the size of the squares increased. (Obviously, the fourth side would still remain unmeasured, but it would be an interesting investigation to pursue because it highlights how all squares are similar.) She also predicted that as the size of the squares increased, the amount of string left over from using three diagonals would also increase. Her findings provided a beginning discussion of the idea that all squares, just like circles, are similar. Increase

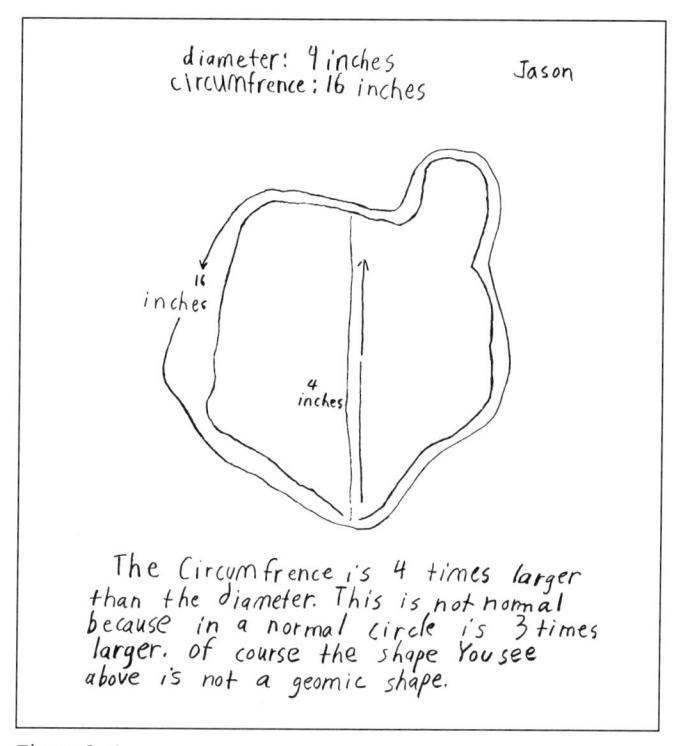

> diameter: 4 inches
> circumfrence: 16 inches   Jason
>
> [drawing of irregular blob shape with 16 inches across and 4 inches vertical]
>
> The Circumfrence is 4 times larger than the diameter. This is not normal because in a normal circle is 3 times larger. of course the shape you see above is not a geomic shape.

Figure 3–6

in the length of sides would give a proportionate increase in the length of diagonals. Understanding similarity in polygons was a fifth-grade objective. Robin saw Melissa's investigation as a natural context for discussing this idea with the class.

Other children explored triangles. Brent looked for a 3:1 ratio in a variety of triangles (Figure 3–7) and found that "regular size" triangles came closer to exhibiting this ratio than "slimmer triangles." Brent was not content to measure just one kind of triangle, but pushed himself to test a variety of examples before making any conclusions. He also used his own language of "regular" and "slimmer" to describe the triangles rather than the technical terms of "equilateral" and "isosceles." Again, this was another instance of children using their own language to describe key attributes and relationships. By continuing to legitimize their language, we kept building a community where all voices are heard and respected. (We did discuss the more conventional terms with the children later on.)

Lindsay G. drew similar triangles and found that three heights almost "stretched" around the perimeter (Figure 3–8). Her conclusion that "if the triangle gets bigger the gap gets bigger" was similar to the finding that the children had noted about circles that increased in size. In their own language they were describing the concept of proportionality and were connecting circles and triangles in a unique way. Shapes that are similar, whether they be circles or triangles, grow

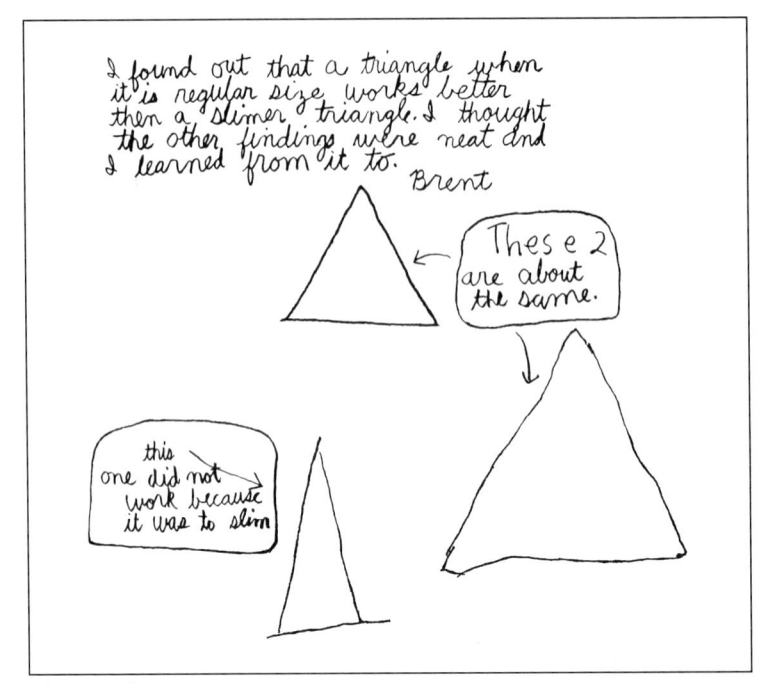

Figure 3–7

in proportionate ways. When Lindsay G. shared her drawings with the class many students found her use of letters to label the gaps to be very interesting. Lindsay G. said she merely wanted to make a "graph" to show her results, and her line lengths reminded her of a graphical representation. Thus, the children were not only sharing the content of their findings with each other but also demonstrating alternative ways to display their data. In fact, her symbolic representation of line segments demonstrated a beginning application of algebraic thinking, an important aspect of fifth-grade mathematics.

During the class discussion several children found rectangles that exhibited this 3:1 ratio while others found rectangles that did not (they were using the length of the rectangle as the unit of measure to stretch around the perimeter). One of the rectangles that satisfied this 3:1 ratio was the following:

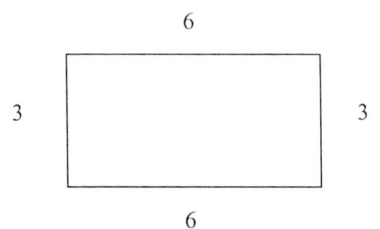

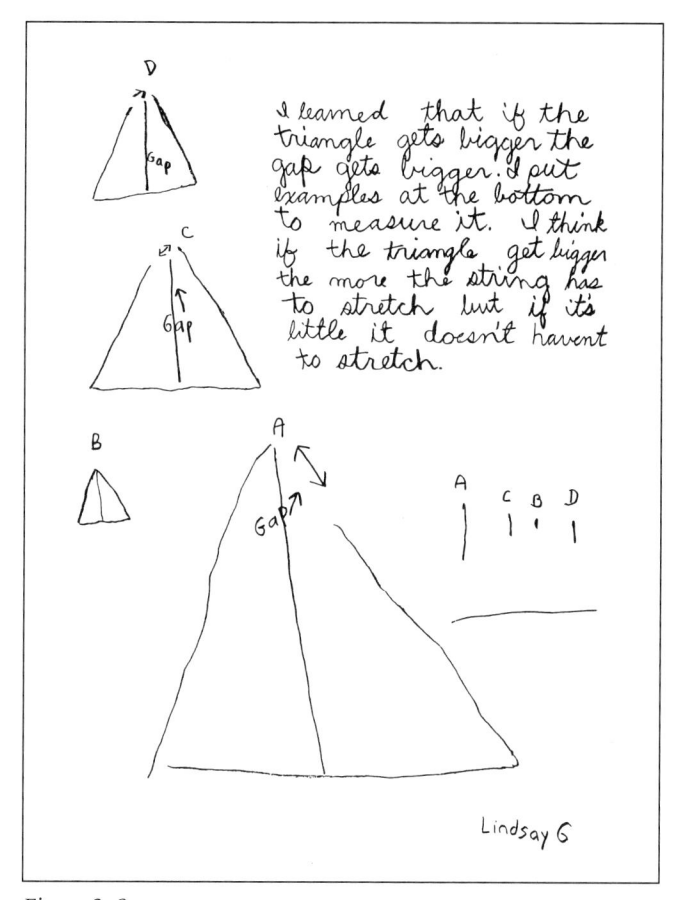

Figure 3–8

The children shared other rectangles that met this 3:1 ratio, such as a 1 × 2 and a 2 × 4. As they reviewed these results they noted that there was a 2:1 ratio between the length and the width of these rectangles. This insight enabled them to generate other possible dimensions for rectangles that would work, such as a 4 × 8, 5 × 10, 6 × 12, and so on. Lindsay G. described the relationship of width to length as "doubling" and Amanda explained it in the opposite way: "I learned that when you have a rectangle you can measure it by half." The descriptions of doubling and halving provided two ways to view the relationship. These explorations also addressed several of the fifth-grade math standards, including the concepts of ratio, similarity, and the skill of determining the perimeter of polygons.

Important learning can occur when mathematicians are encouraged to go beyond the data. However, that learning can happen only in an inquiry environment that respects ideas, values risk taking, and recognizes the social nature of learning. These conditions of inquiry are evident in some of the children's reflections written at the conclusion of this investigation. Tennille commented on how the language of the community helped her grow: "I learned that when you hear other people share what they did you find new ways to say things." Jennifer recognized how one idea generates other ideas: "When I saw other people work, that made me think about other things I could work with." Talitha wrote about risk taking and the respect for each other's ideas: "I learned that if you try you can do anything. And if you listen to others they can listen to you." Robin believed that children could support each other in taking risks. Therefore, she conducted regular sharing times before, during, and after an investigation. She encouraged children to share plans or ideas that they were not quite sure about, but were interested in pursuing. For instance, "Brent isn't sure if this 3:1 ratio will work with triangles, so he is testing out different sized triangles." Robin felt that publicly acknowledging risk-taking ventures would encourage others to do some experimenting, too.

When mathematicians go beyond the data, they generate new insights. Jason's question enabled the children to investigate the relationship between the diagonal and side lengths of a square and to develop a beginning understanding of how all squares are similar. The children also noted how triangles could also grow in proportionate ways. They found that special rectangles whose length-to-width ratio was 2:1 showed a length-to-perimeter ratio of 3:1. It was this problem posing by Jason that opened the door for these new explorations and demonstrated to the class that no investigation is ever finished. Instead, new answers, such as this 3:1 ratio for circles, simply provide more data for children to extend and modify in new ways.

Mathematicians Create Their Own Language

Mathematicians, like any group of explorers, often use their own language to describe what they have discovered. Generating their own mathematical terms and definitions builds a sense of community by strengthening individual voices. It also challenges children to draw upon their current mathematical understandings in creating this language (Rubenstein and Schwartz 2000; Rubenstein 1996). The children raised one question about language when they shared their findings about other shapes. They described their measuring unit of string as "a diameter," since that was the term we had used with circles. Charlie wondered whether we ought to be calling these other interior lines "diameters," since only circles have diameters. (Spheres also have diameters, as the children discovered in reading the dictionary definition later on.) The class agreed that they ought to use another word, so we urged them to create their own. Together we looked at the etymologies of some of the mathematical words we had been using, and then invited the children to create their own word. The children copied our findings in their journal (Figure 3–9) and then decided together that "dia-rectus" would nicely fit their needs, since they reasoned it would mean "straight through."

We also asked the children to create their own definitions of a circle. We were curious to see what particular features of a circle they would include, given their

Mathematicians Create Their Own Language 51

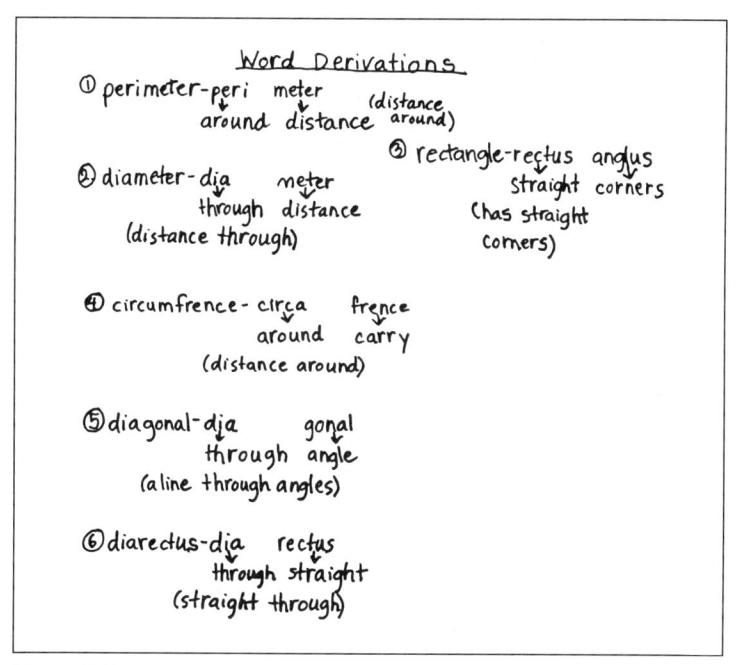

```
                    Word Derivations
    ① perimeter - peri    meter       (distance
                 around  distance      around)
                                    ③ rectangle - rectus  angus
    ② diameter - dia     meter                  straight  corners
                through  distance              (has straight
                (distance through)              corners)


    ④ circumfrence - circa   frence
                    around   carry
                    (distance around)

    ⑤ diagonal - dia      gonal
                through   angle
                (a line through angles)

    ⑥ diarectus - dia    rectus
                through  straight
                (straight through)
```

Figure 3–9

recent experiences with circles. As the children shared their definitions they tried to revise each other's descriptions by noting certain unique features of their own:

TENNILLE: It is round shaped with curved lines.

MELISSA B.:   They might get it mixed up and think it is a sphere, if you don't say it is flat. I said it was a round, flat object.

Lindsay G.:   It is a round, flat shape with no points or corners. The lines do not turn in.

CHARLIE: You could still draw an oval.

MELISSA E.:   When you draw an oval, it stretches out. It is a round object not a sphere, no sides, all one size [unlike an oval] all around.

LEE: A line that curves until it gets to where it started.

NIGEL: No wrinkles in it. It's not steep. It doesn't go up too much.

LEE: At one point that oval has straight lines.

MELISSA B.:   It is kind of like a ball with no air in it.

LINDSAY B.:   If it has straight lines it can't be a circle. It is perfectly round, curves the same all around. Curves the same amount wherever it goes.

ROBERT: Only one diameter that is the same length through the center.

Here again the children assume a skeptical stance toward each other's definitions, and work together to revise the overall definition as the conversation unfolds. Mathematicians debate and challenge in a constructive, respectful way. Paradoxically, it is in disagreement that we become a closer community of mathematical thinkers. What counts in this class is thinking; part of that thinking involves being skeptical, raising questions, and suggesting alternatives. Such challenges are not done in a derogatory or spiteful way. Instead, children raise questions with a thoughtful and sincere intent. Mathematicians thrive in an environment in which ideas are the currency of conversation (Hiebert 1997), and individual voices are heard and respected.

It is interesting to note how the children's definitions in this group discussion differed from the standard definition of a circle that would be found in their textbook or dictionary (i.e., a circle is a plane figure bounded by a single curved line, every point of which is equally distant from the point at the center of the figure). First, the children distinguished a circle from other shapes, such as ovals and spheres. These comparisons enriched their understanding of not only circles, but other shapes as well. We felt Melissa B.'s definition of a circle as a squished sphere was extremely insightful, drawing a unique parallel between two-dimensional and three-dimensional figures. Second, the children often listed the features of a circle in a negative way, such as "no sides," "no wrinkles," and "it's not steep." Recognizing the non-attributes of a shape also helped learners distinguish it from other shapes. Third, the children captured some of the main characteristics of a circle in a succinct, poetic way: for example, "A line that curves until it gets to where it started," and "Curves are the same amount wherever it goes." In addition, this experience addressed the fifth-grade skill of comparing and classifying polygons in different ways.

We then asked the children, "Why was it important that we create our own definitions for a circle? Wouldn't it have been easier and quicker to read and learn a definition from your textbook?" We asked these questions because we wanted the children to share with us the value they saw in this experience. We also knew that to build an inquiry classroom, we needed to invite the children to reflect on our decisions as teachers. Part of building a community is making our intentions as teachers explicit to our students. Their perspective on classroom events helps us grow as teachers. Their responses were quite revealing:

LEE: We couldn't explore it. We wouldn't learn everyone else's and couldn't explore it.

NIGEL: I would have to depend on someone else when I grow up.

MELISSA B.: I would have to depend on the book and I couldn't make up my own things and learn from myself.

JENNY: You need to learn what other people think too and not just the book.

LINDSAY B.: You can make up your own definition that no one even thought of.

JENNY: So you can see what other people think. Your thinking makes other people think.

LINDSAY G.: If you learn from your own resources you wouldn't have to learn from a book all the time.

BRANDON: One day you may want to be on *Jeopardy*.

The children realized that they are empowered learners when they construct knowledge in their own way. As a community we were learning how to help learners to think for themselves. Our conversations with children were affirming for us once again the importance of viewing children as sense makers and respecting their individual interpretations.

Going Beyond the Experience

As we reflected on this experience as teachers, we thought about the important lessons we could bring to future investigations. Following are some of these strategies:

1. Invite children to write their own definitions of mathematical concepts and ideas. We chose circles. You might choose other geometric shapes, or concepts such as ratio, average, odd and even numbers, and so on. Children can share their definitions in small groups and then develop a collaborative definition.

2. Postpone technical vocabulary until later in a mathematical exploration. Give the children time to explain a term in their own way first by engaging them in experiences that require the use of these mathematical ideas. Topics such as prime and composite numbers, similarity, and congruence might be explored in this way.

3. Encourage children to look for patterns (even when no patterns seem evident). It is important for children to make predictions about patterns, describe them, and explain why they are occurring.

4. Encourage children to write about the ideas of their classmates in their journals and discuss how these ideas stirred their own thinking (Whitin and Whitin 2000). Children can share these recognitions aloud and then post them on an ongoing wall chart entitled, "Mathematical Thinkers Help Each Other Grow."

5. Support children's skepticism of mathematical findings. Ask, "What part of these findings did you expect? What parts did you *not* expect? What parts seem unlikely, or difficult to believe?" Use this doubt as a way for the whole class to test further examples or to investigate the same idea in other ways.

6. Invite children to reflect on the discussions you conduct as a teacher.

For instance, you might ask, "Why do you suppose we had such a long discussion today about how you use estimation in your everyday life? Why didn't we start by just reading about estimation in a book?"

7. Encourage children to go beyond the data by asking, "Now that we have made these discoveries, what are you wondering about now?" Their wonders often lead to further directions—pursuits that can often be assigned as homework.

4 Mathematicians Are Problem Solvers Who Invent Their Own Tools

Mathematicians are inventors. They invent tools to solve problems and to make life easier. For instance, they invent the multiplication algorithm so that they do not have to add 23 fifteen times. They invent generalizations so they do not have to test all possible cases, such as the formula of $L \times W$ to represent the area calculation for any rectangle. They invent tangible tools, such as a compass, scale, or calculator. Inventing is part of the mathematical legacy. In this chapter we describe a mathematical experience in which children invented tools for calculating the areas of irregular shapes. Not only did we want to support them in developing these tools, but we also wanted to build upon some of their previous experiences. For instance, the children's work with pumpkins and circles involved such concepts as length (i.e., perimeter and circumference), volume, weight, and ratio. These experiences provided a rich groundwork from which to explore more deeply the relationship between perimeter and area. We knew it was a relationship that seemed a bit puzzling even for adults (Walter 1970)—that is, how shapes with the same perimeter can have different areas. Therefore, we wanted to provide the children with a hands-on experience that would allow them to investigate these concepts in their own way.

Robin had experienced this same investigation as a learner a few years earlier when David W. introduced it as part of a graduate course. She sensed the potential of the experience for her children and wanted to give them this opportunity. We had also learned from the exploration with circles that it was important for children to create their own definitions and invent their own strategies for solving problems. We wanted to continue to nurture this same spirit of invention and exploration. We had learned that it was crucial to keep the experience open-ended so that children had a chance to interpret the problem in various ways. We tried to keep these important lessons in mind as we created the following lesson plan. Robin also mentioned that the children would be taking a field trip to Charleston, South Carolina, later in the year, and she felt this experience with perimeter and area would provide the children with a mathematical lens for thinking about why people build houses in the shapes that they do.

Lesson Plan and Intended Outcomes

Lesson Plan	Intended Outcomes—Process	Intended Outcomes—Product
Challenge the children to find shapes with large areas. (30 minutes)	Children offer a variety of answers and interpretations to this open-ended task.	Children explore the relationship between area and perimeter.
Conduct a class discussion on initial findings, focusing on one child's shapes as a common referent for all to consider. (30 minutes)	Children use their own language to describe the concepts of perimeter and area.	Children estimate areas of irregular polygons.
Present the next challenge: How can we be sure that one shape has a larger area than another? What tools could we invent to compare them? (20 minutes)	Children take risks to share possibilities as they justify their reasoning and build upon each other's ideas.	Children devise nonstandard units to measure area.
Children test out tools, calculate areas of irregular shapes, and keep records of their results. (40 minutes)	Children draw upon the group's ideas to develop their own plan of action. They represent their findings in their own way.	Children use nonstandard units to calculate the area of irregular shapes.
Children reflect on the experience. (20 minutes)	Children share conclusions with peers and pose other questions for future investigations.	Children understand the need for a standard unit.

Starting the Investigation

We began our exploration by reading aloud *The Village of Round and Square Houses* (1986) by Ann Grifalconi. It is a lovely African tale that describes the cultural reasons for men living in square houses and women living in round ones. Later on, we asked the children to think of other reasons for building houses in particular shapes. These included: (1) the kind of materials available, such as wood, mud or bamboo; (2) the kind of lifestyles people lead, such as whether they are nomadic or more permanent dwellers; (3) the weather; (4) personal taste; and (5) cost and availability of building materials. These reasons provided a contextual framework for thinking about architectural styles.

Next we gave each person a piece of string 34 centimeters long and a piece of paper and described the following challenge: "Pretend that you live in a society in which people produce almost everything they need by their own efforts. Your family is planning to build a house. You and your family must gather all the materials, perhaps with the help of your neighbors. Some of the materials may be hard to come by, and you want to use as little as possible. Pretend that you have collected a certain amount of material for the walls (the piece of string). Figure out what shape will give you the largest floor space with this quantity of material" (Zaslavsky 1989).

The children spent one class session (one hour) creating some shapes and discussing their initial findings with the whole class. They spent another session brainstorming possible tools for calculating the areas of these irregular shapes so they could know for sure which shapes yielded the largest possible areas. During the final class session they tested one of these tools, recorded their findings, and shared their results with the class. Throughout this process we assessed the children's understanding of the mathematical concepts involved and their proficiency in using any mathematical skills they employed (adding decimals, rounding, comparing fractions, etc.). For instance, as children contributed ideas during meetings (or to us privately as we talked with them at their desks) or recorded ideas in their journals, we asked ourselves: Who seems to understand the relationship between perimeter and area? Who understands that the circle yields the largest possible area, and why this is so? Who understands the limits and potentials of various measuring tools? Who accurately computes their answers? Who understands that shapes with the same perimeter can yield different areas? Some of the children's oral and written responses in this chapter highlight a few of these questions that we posed for ourselves.

The First Day: Examining the Potato and the Squash

After the children had constructed irregular shapes with a variety of obvious areas, we held a class meeting to discuss their initial findings. We decided to focus the discussion on two shapes that Erin had created, which she had named the "potato" and the "squash" (Figure 4–1). We had circulated around the room during this first work time, observing the children and listening to their reasoning. We

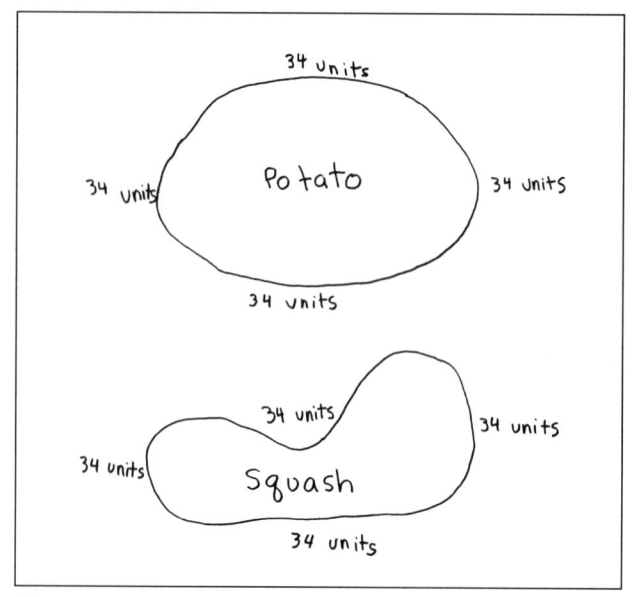

Figure 4–1

felt that Erin's work would provide an interesting comparison for all to consider because the shapes appeared to be fairly close in area. She had placed centimeter cubes around the edge of each shape and confirmed for herself that the distance around each one was 34 centimeters. We drew larger versions of her shapes on the board so everyone could see the shapes more clearly. We felt that by focusing on one child's work we could keep the discussion more centered and still highlight their understanding of area. Although most children estimated visually and concluded that the "potato" shape appeared to cover more area, others were not so sure. We asked all the children to explain their reasoning so that their thinking was made public for the class to consider. The following class conversation highlights facets of a collaborative community of inquirers: taking risks by proposing different explanations for comparing the areas; offering slightly different interpretations of the problem; and describing the distinction between perimeter and area in various ways.

David W. initiated the conversation by asking, "Look at the two shapes that Erin created. Which of these two shapes do you think would give you the most area to run around in?" The children's comments helped us assess their understanding of perimeter and area. For instance, Kelvin opened the discussion by arguing that both shapes had the same area: "I think it's the same because they are both 34. If you move the line of that squash up, it would be like the potato, so they would both be the same." He was arguing since the perimeters were 34, then the areas could also be the same if the string were moved. Derek reiterated this point when he said, "If you stretch out the squash it would probably be the same [area as the potato]." Later on we wondered whether Kelvin and Derek were arguing that they could make the areas equal *only* because the perimeters were equal. We were not entirely sure. What would have happened if we had asked them both to construct two shapes with the same area but different perimeters?

Assuming this reflective stance makes us better teachers and more careful listeners of our students. Thus, the children's comments gave us a window into their thinking, but it was not always a clear window. We were making assumptions about what we thought they meant but we could not fully assess their understanding until we talked with them further or provided additional experiences. We have found that this kind of ongoing assessment sometimes raises more questions than it answers. However, as inquirers ourselves, this seemed inevitable. Just as our students were inquiring into the relationship between perimeter and area, we were inquiring into the children's reasoning and sense-making efforts. Just as we support our students in posing further questions to investigate, we too plan extension experiences to answer our next questions. We were realizing anew that we were all inquirers together.

We have also come to realize that giving children regular opportunities to explain their reasoning can often lead to alternative interpretations of the problem. This occurred later in the conversation when Kelvin observed that both shapes had exterior as well as interior space: "Maybe the potato is bigger on the inside but the squash is bigger on the outside, if they have the same amount of line" (Figure 4–2). This distinction between interior and exterior space was a new way to view the problem. Since the children had drawn these figures on 8½ × 11 sheets

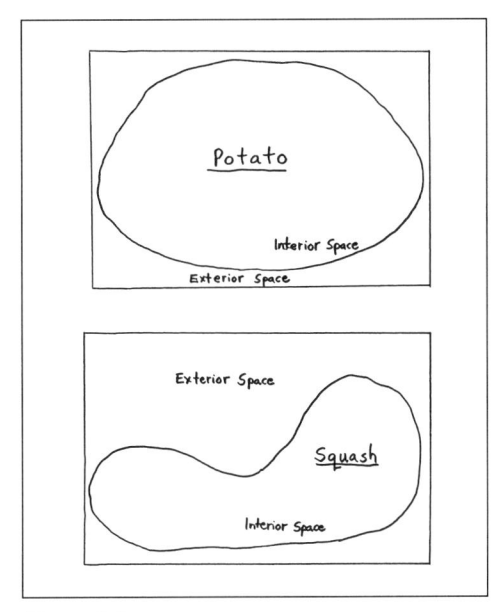

Figure 4–2

of paper that had definite borders, it was only natural to describe these two types of spaces. Kelvin's observation was hinting at an inverse relationship, that is, the more interior space a shape contains, the less exterior space it occupies, and visa versa. We did not have time to pursue this point with the children, but it intrigued us as teachers nonetheless. We surmised that many architectural decisions are based on the utilization of the interior (housing) and exterior (landscaping) spaces on a given plot of land. Robin realized that the children could examine this relationship during their trip to Charleston later in the year. Kelvin's comment helped to demonstrate once again how open-ended explorations can stretch the thinking of students and teachers alike.

The discussion also highlighted the unique personal connections that the children made with the concept of area. Brandon used his familiarity with football to discuss the difference between the potato and the squash: "I think the potato because it has more room in it. Like say you want to play football. The squash you can just run straight, but the potato has more room up." Later on, when discussing the difference between a square and a rectangle, he made the same comparison: "It's like when you play football. The rectangle is longer, and it might tire you out more than the square. The square gives you more out-of-bounds space." His knowledge of a football playing field helped him analyze Erin's two shapes; although we had talked earlier of a square and a rectangle having the same perimeter, Brandon argued that if both shapes were used for football, the rectangle would be more tiring to run around in. Chris had made this point earlier when he remarked, "It depends on what you want to do on the inside. You need different shapes for different things." His comment helped the class think about the purpose of a given space and underscored the importance of context in interpreting this problem.

As fellow learners in this classroom community, we teachers also learned an important lesson about language. We recognized that the original problem challenged the children to figure out what shape would yield the largest possible floor space with this fixed amount of material. However, when we listened to this taped conversation later on, we realized that David W. described the problem as "the most area to run around in." Although he intended to use this language to make the concept of area more accessible to students, he unknowingly changed the context of the problem. The description of "run-around space" conjured up other associations for students. Brandon and others argued that the potato shape was the more appropriate solution because it was closest to a football field, a familiar space that related to running around. Aaron also picked up on David W.'s language and argued that if one were to run around the edges of each shape, the answers would be equivalent: "If you run around the edge of each one, it would still be 34 for each." As teachers we were learning that the language we use influences the interpretations of these problems by our students. We reflected later that we needed to clarify this distinction between running around the edge of each shape and running around in the interior space. We also felt we should have returned to the context of the original problem and emphasized "the largest floor space" for a family house. However, we did not realize this language issue until much later, when we analyzed the taped conversation in more detail. Nonetheless, even in hindsight, we learned some important lessons:

1. The language we use to frame a mathematical problem influences the interpretations that our students construct.

2. When students offer alternative interpretations from the ones that we expect, listen closely to their language. The language of the problem, and their personal associations with that language, shape their interpretations.

3. It is important to share these insights about language with our students. In this way they, too, can be more reflective about how language influences their problem-solving efforts. Such sharing builds a sense of community as teacher and student together reflect on the process of how we learn. It also underscores for our students the idea that language plays a key role in mathematical problem solving.

4. The role of context shapes the decisions that we make as problem solvers. Deciding the best area for playing football is a different problem from determining the most area for a house. Another example is sharing twelve cookies among three children, which might yield different answers depending upon whether these children are close school friends or younger siblings.

Another benefit of this initial conversation was the language that the children used to describe these various areas. For instance, Leslie said, "I think the potato shape [is larger] because it's long and wide. The squash shape is long but not that wide." She knew to consider both dimensions for area. She aptly borrowed the language of "length" and "width" that she was probably accustomed to using for rectangles and applied it to these irregular shapes. Cole described the shapes in a more physical way: "The potato has a lot of space to run around in it, but the squash has more places scrunched together. And if you tried to play something, like football, you'd have all these walls near you." David W. even extended the idea by saying, "Yes, you'd be very cramped." It is words such as *long*, *wide*, *scrunched*, and *cramped* that enrich the collective understanding of the concept of area. As a fixed perimeter is made into different shapes, it creates different kinds of spaces for various activities. The children were describing these spaces in their own way. Drawing out children's language to describe these mathematical ideas legitimizes their thinking and grants them a sense of ownership and personal connection to the task.

Throughout the initial conversation children also kept offering reasons why two shapes could have the same perimeter but different areas. Some claimed that it was possible to create different shapes because they could be "stretched," and these shapes had different lengths, widths, and angles. David G. tried to summarize his classmates' ideas by offering this relationship: "When you make a round shape there's more space in the middle, but when you make a longer shape there's less in the middle." His description nicely reflects what happens as a fixed perimeter moves from its least to its greatest area.

Lauren extended this discussion of perimeter and area in still another way by relating it to squares and rectangles: "Like if you had a rectangle that was 34 units all the way around, and a square that was 34 units, it's not the same shape, but it's still the same . . . size [perimeter]. It's just not the same shape." David G. was intrigued by this idea and predicted, "I think the square would be bigger around [i.e., fatter] but the rectangle would be bigger longer [i.e., more narrow]." As the children explored this relationship later, they did indeed find that, with the same perimeter, a square occupied more space than a rectangle.

Developing Tools for Calculating the Area

Children soon realized that they needed some way to measure the areas of their shapes. Only then would they know for sure which shapes were the largest, and by how much. In the last part of this conversation the children began to suggest possible tools for calculating these areas. David W. had discussed with Robin a lesson he had learned about the importance of children developing these tools for themselves. He had planned this same experience with another group of fifth-grade students several years earlier and had given centimeter paper to the children right away so they could calculate the area (Whitin 1993). Even when he had provided grid paper, several students still seemed puzzled about how those squares were going to help them calculate the area. When David W. told them to count the squares, he realized that he was not really helping them learn about the concept of area. Although the children's insights about the experience were quite valuable, David W. felt he had robbed the children of some fruitful learning opportunities by providing them with a single tool (centimeter paper) right away. David W. has learned that when he tells children how to solve a problem, he is not fostering resourceful problem solvers. NCTM supports the development of problem solvers who are encouraged to draw upon their own knowledge to create new mathematical understandings. It advocates that students have "frequent opportunities to formulate, grapple with, and solve complex problems that require a significant amount of effort" (2000, p. 52). Learning experiences ought to be structured so that students "acquire ways of thinking, habits of persistence and curiosity, and confidence in unfamiliar situations" (2000, p. 52). For these reasons, David W. suggested to Robin that they not use centimeter paper, forcing children to discuss the concept of area in their own way and devise an appropriate tool for calculating it.

Since the children had used the base 10 blocks for more than a month, they began to think of how they could use that material as a measuring tool. Bobby suggested using flats, longs, and units to fill a given area. Chris began to note the relationship between volume and area when he said, "If the square was a cube, you layer." He was learning to see area as the bottom layer of a volume calculation. Having a variety of mathematical models in a classroom, such as base 10 blocks, provides learners with visual images of the mathematical system and allows them to make these important connections between concepts. When we asked the children how they could use square units to measure a curved edge, they offered a variety of strategies:

CRYSTAL: You could say two of those little [extra] spaces make one whole square.

COLE: Just keep putting a lot of little bits together to make a whole.

DAVID G.: You could draw a little line to show what is left over [i.e., what part of the base 10 block extends beyond the outline of the shape], and then put that leftover space somewhere else.

As the discussion continued, the children suggested a variety of strategies for adapting the tool of base 10 blocks to calculate the area of irregular figures:

- counting half pieces
- counting several pieces to make a whole
- counting full squares that partially fall outside the edge, then later subtracting that extra amount from the interior region

Their strategies helped to show that there were multiple ways to solve a given problem, and contributed to our growing sense of a mathematical community.

The children also suggested using various pattern blocks and we raised the possibility of using buttons. We saw part of our role as suggesting other materials but in a nonjudgmental way, letting the children debate the merits of each one. We have found that nothing shuts down conversations more than our granting approval for one method over another. We undermine the children's own autonomy and decision making when we decide which approach is best. We try to suspend judgment and allow the children to evaluate and test their ideas. However, that is not to say that we remove ourselves from the debate completely. We believe another important teaching role is to summarize the children's findings so that the pros and cons of each strategy are made clear.

Erin argued that buttons would be an appropriate measuring tool because their rounded edge would better fit the curved edges of the irregular shapes. However, Melanie did not agree because "buttons are different shapes, and when you will fill up the inside of your shape you can't tell how much it is." She recognized that a measuring unit needed to be uniform in size. Bobby also felt that buttons might not be an appropriate measuring tool, but for a different reason: "If these are circles, there are little open spaces and they won't fit together. So if you filled up your space with fifty-one circles, it would probably be more because there's space open. It might be more like sixty-one because you have to put all those spaces together, and it would add up to be more." Bobby recognized that buttons, or other circles, would not be an accurate measure because they do not tessellate (cover a plane completely without any gaps or overlapping). Thus, both children showed some important conceptual understanding of measurement tools, that is, they must tessellate and be uniform in size. These are the kind of basic understandings that children must grapple with when they are given the opportunity to devise their own tools for measuring.

Finally, Chris concluded that no measuring tool would cover an irregular shape completely, and remarked, "No matter what shape we use, we're still going to have little spaces that we can't fill up." His comment underscores the notion that all measurements are approximations. Irregular shapes readily demonstrate this idea. However, even the more familiar squares and rectangles are not without their approximate value; that is, whatever the size of the measurement unit we use, we could always select a smaller one to be even more precise.

Richie then suggested using water because of its unique property "to move into any shape." At this point Bobby recommended that certain measuring tools be used for certain shapes, such as squares to cover rectangles but a more rounded or oval shape to cover the area of a circular object. The children were confronting the inherent difficulties in calculating the area of irregular shapes.

In summary, this class conversation allowed the children to explore some important mathematical ideas: (1) the relationship between perimeter and area; (2) the property of certain shapes to tessellate a plane; and (3) the constraints and possibilities of certain discrete (base 10 blocks, pattern blocks) and continuous (water) materials for covering an irregular area.

On the next day the children expanded on some of these earlier ideas for measuring and explored some new ones. Richie again suggested the tool of water to address the difficulties of measuring around a curved perimeter: "You could just get some water and drop it in, and see how much it fills up." David W. and Robin were intrigued with this idea of using a continuous material, such as water, and David W. built upon Richie's idea: "So maybe you could create your own shape using aluminum foil. Then turn the edges up so it would be like a cup. And then we could drop the water in there." However, Chris challenged this idea: "If you fold the aluminum foil, the edges would take up space, and the shape wouldn't be as big." David W. realized Chris had a good point: "You're right. You would have to make that shape a bit bigger. Then you could fold it up so it would be your exact shape." Robin then argued that the shapes would have to be filled up at the same height so that the comparison was fair. Cole then issued another caution: "I think you need to put the water in gently, so you don't make any bubbles [which would occupy some of the measurable space]." Again, to make a valid comparison this measuring tool of water needed to be used consistently.

This first part of the discussion reflects some of the inquiry conditions that Robin had been trying to promote in her classroom. Building a community is one of these conditions. Here students and teachers are learners together. Richie's marvelous idea of using water as a measuring tool for irregular shapes began the conversation. His suggestion was one that had never occurred to us teachers, and

David W. excitedly built upon Richie's idea by suggesting the use of aluminum foil. In hindsight David W. wondered whether he should have refrained from sharing this idea and instead turned the problem back to Richie by asking, "Say some more about how we could use water to measure these shapes." In this way children retain more ownership for working out the details for a particular solution. However, there were benefits in his response as well. He was clearly demonstrating that he was a learner too, and that one idea often leads to another in a collaborative community. We have learned that there are a variety of ways to value children's ideas and build a sense of community.

The remainder of the conversation was comprised of Chris' challenge to the size of the aluminum cups, and Robin's and Cole's caveats about the height of the water and the number of bubbles. Communities thrive on such challenges and debate. However, the tone of that debate is the critical factor. If the tone of the language is sarcastic or demeaning, then an aura of disrespect undermines the very community that we are trying to establish. We have found that we have to heed this tone, and not just the language itself, if we want to build a community that nurtures the voices of all the children.

The discussion continued about other possible tools for measuring the areas of these irregular shapes. Erin suggested, "Maybe we could use mustard and fill the bottom of the shapes." David W. responded, "Yes, I suppose that we could use anything like that . . . but your idea about the mustard makes me think about something else we could use to fit into the corners, like clay." Lauren then suggested some strategies for measuring these lumps of clay: "We could weigh it, or we could cut squares into the clay by pressing down a flat from the base 10 blocks." Melanie liked the latter idea because "the squares have to be the same size, so you're counting the same thing."

As we reflect on this previous conversation, we see more instances of children and adults building on each other's ideas. For instance, when Erin suggested mustard, many of the children giggled. However, it was her suggestion of a substance that could easily fit into the contours of an irregular shape that prompted David W. to suggest clay. And even before David W. could think through how clay could be used to compare two given areas, Lauren chimed in with some ideas on how to use the clay as a tool for measuring. In this way each idea provided a beginning point for new ideas and possibilities.

We have found that some of the most generative mathematical discussions come when we withhold judgment on each other's ideas and refrain from coming to some consensus about their worthiness. It would have been tempting to tell Erin not to suggest messy items like mustard and to treat the discussion "more seriously." However, part of the reason we accepted her contribution was that we knew Erin well. She was a freethinker who often suggested different solutions to problems. Sometimes children offer such answers to gain attention for themselves. Although Erin enjoyed the attention for her alternative approach, she was serious about her suggestion. Mustard was certainly an appropriate solution for filling in the irregular contours of the children's shapes. In fact, later in the conversation when the idea of creating a more permanent mold of a given area was raised, Erin suggested using Jell-O. Her idea capitalized on two key attributes of gelatin—it could fill the irregular contours of the shapes (like water) and, when firm, provide a permanent cast of that shape for further measuring.

Her suggestion of gelatin led Bobby to suggest plaster of paris as a possibility, which several of the children did use during the next part of the investigation. They made casts of the given areas and then weighed them as a basis for comparing their areas. The point is that withholding judgment on Erin's seemingly outlandish ideas led to some more feasible tools, such as clay and plaster of paris. We were careful to recognize Erin for her contributions: "Erin, your idea about mustard made me think about something else that could fit into the corners, like clay." We had clay in the classroom and we all knew (including Erin) it would be easier to use. However, we walk a fine line as teachers. We want to build a community that encourages children to take risks, share alternative solutions, and demonstrate different ways of thinking. But how do we know when children are using these norms to benefit themselves and not the group? When are children suggesting ideas to be funny, draw attention to themselves, or purposely derail the conversation so that no time is left to complete the task? Despite our best efforts at building a community, we have all had children with such intentions. The problem then becomes, what do we do when children suggest seemingly far-out solutions? As we mentioned earlier, one guideline we follow is: Know your children. We knew Erin was serious and we accepted her contribution. Another strategy that we have found useful is to have the child explain further details of the solution: "Say some more about how that idea might work." Often their lack of details makes it apparent that their idea would not be practical. It is certainly a difficult issue, and one we continue to grapple with as we strive to build collaborative communities of inquirers.

Testing Their Measuring Tools

Before the children actually chose a tool for their measuring we asked them to comment in their journal about any part of the previous conversation. We find it useful for children to reflect on group conversations because it validates discussions as an important part of our community, and it enables us to hear the voices of all children (some of whom did not contribute during the conversation). Brandi captured many of her classmates' feelings when she commented about the advantages and disadvantages of certain materials (Figure 4–3). She thought the continuous materials would be more effective because water "takes up all the room" and clay "will always be there" (i.e., it will provide a permanent record as well as fit around the contours). She disliked the idea of using pattern blocks or base 10 blocks because they would "not go around the sides and it will leave holes." Thus, when the children were given some time to explore using various materials, the most popular items included plaster of paris, clay, and water. The majority of the children found that, indeed, the circle

> When we were talking about witch one would show which one has more room inside. I was think witch ones would work better to show that. Well, I think that the clay is a good idea because it will always be there. The alum. foil and water is also a very good idea because water takes up all the room and you can tell it better. The patt. block, units, flats, and longs I think will not work because in a circle it will not go around the side and it will leave holes. Now, to the plaster. I think it will do a great job at what we are doing. It is messy but it will let us have fun and find the ansewr to are question. What do I think about the string. I think that it is the way that you pull or push the string together.
>
> —Brandi

Figure 4–3

yielded the largest possible area, but they arrived at this conclusion in a variety of ways.

A Window into One Child's Thinking

Robin met with several groups of children to make molds of their shapes using plaster of paris. The other children worked individually or in pairs to test some other materials. Cole decided to compare his two shapes by measuring across each one at different locations (Figure 4–4). He wrote those measurements on the outside of each. He then added these different measurements, intending to compare the two sums. His strategy combined part of what he knew about perimeter (using a linear measurement) and part of what he knew about area (the need to measure *across* a given space, not around). He used inches as his measuring unit and recorded the number of marks beyond the inch line in the decimal place. (His totals for each figure, 21.5 and 18.7, are not quite accurate). Although he was confusing metric and standard notation, he was aware that the measurements across a given space would be useful in calculating area. In hindsight, it would have been

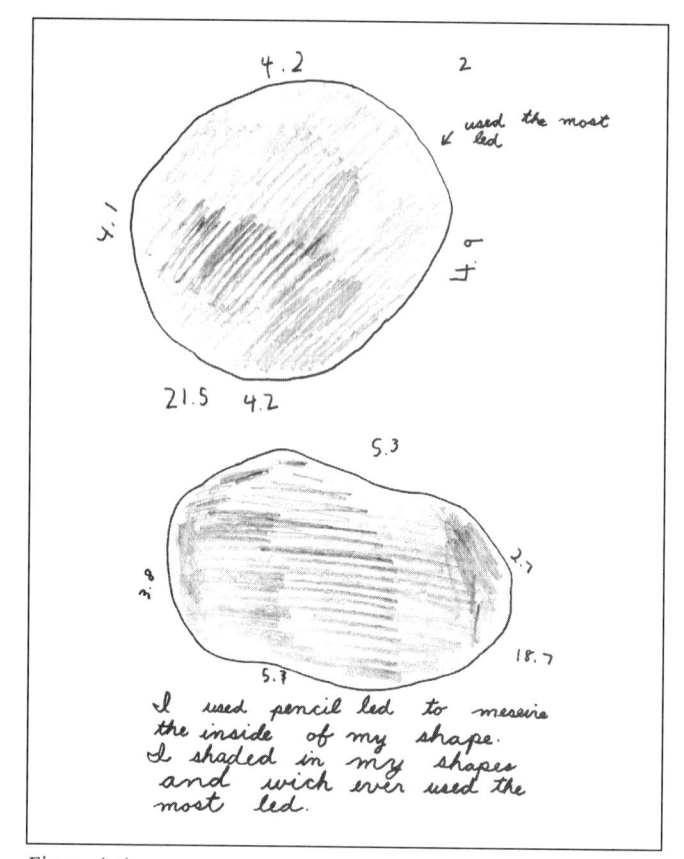

Figure 4–4

helpful to have him test his theory of adding those dimensions using regular shapes. For instance, these two shapes have the same perimeter, but when their lengths and widths are added rather than multiplied, the results are quite different (Figure 4–5). In this way he could see that adding a length and a width yields half the perimeter but it is not useful in determining area.

However, because Cole was not satisfied that his linear measurements were exact, he decided to develop another strategy to compare his shapes. He had noticed the flurry of activity around him as his classmates used a variety of continuous materials, such as water and clay, to fill the edges of their shapes completely. Cole wanted to use a different material, so he decided to fill each shape with pencil lead. He sharpened his pencil for each shape and then carefully shaded in each area; he tried to press down with equal force on each shape and watched to see which area had the lightest shading, indicating the lead was disappearing. He determined that the circular shape used the most lead. He realized his strategy

L = 4
W = 4
4 + 4 = 8
4 x 4 = 16

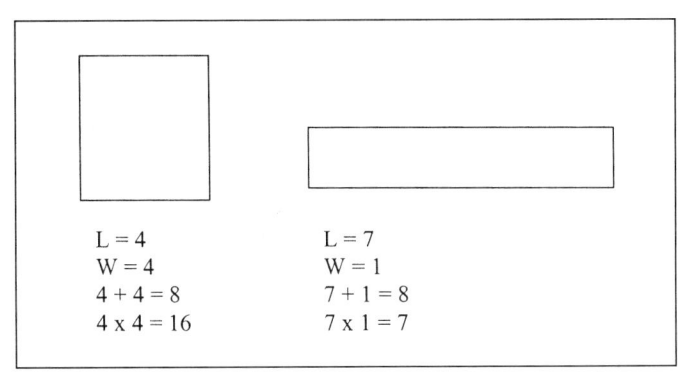

L = 7
W = 1
7 + 1 = 8
7 x 1 = 7

Figure 4–5

was still an estimate, but he was pleased that he could fill the inside of each shape with a continuous material. This second attempt at calculating the areas, although probably not very accurate, helped show us that he knew what the concept of area meant. In his first attempt he was trying to apply what he knew about linear measurement to this new context of area and he was unsure whether his answer made sense. As teachers, we were pleased with both entries. We knew how he was trying to draw upon previous knowledge about perimeters to solve this current problem. We also knew he had a sense of what area means by measuring across his shapes, and then later filling in the shapes with pencil lead. We try to encourage children to solve problems in different ways so that we glimpse their understanding of each method. Cole's example also demonstrates the importance of peers in influencing a child's next steps. Moreover, it highlights how valuable journals can be by revealing how children draw upon previous experiences and how they try to make sense of a new situation. Vygotsky (1978) claims that the best way to assess understanding is to view it in motion. Encouraging children to write, talk, and draw their understandings to open-ended tasks is an important way to view learning in motion.

Calculating the Area Using Water

A group of children used water to fill their shapes. Melanie used aluminum foil to create cups for each of her shapes; she then filled them with water and weighed each one, finding that a circle (27 grams) was heavier (and therefore larger in area) than a squash shape (24 grams). Typically, children in school do not consider using the concept of weight to determine area. However, when experiences are kept open-ended and children are allowed to solve problems in their own way, they often tie concepts together in unique ways. Brandi also found that a circle yielded the greatest area when she compared the number of water drops needed to fill each shape: 140 for the rectangle and 235 for the circle. She had predicted the area of the circle would be greater, and now had a mathematical measure to prove her case.

Lauren used water to compare her shapes (Figure 4–6) and found her squash shape to be slightly larger than her potato shape (her potato shape was more elongated than the one Erin had shared earlier). Her investigation highlighted many of the features of an inquiring community that we were trying hard to establish: (1) She did not settle for a single solution but took a risk at expressing her answer in another way. She compared the area in two different ways: number of drops and number of spoonfuls. (2) She used her own initiative to set the second investigation: "I worked out my problem, then I made up and solved another [one]." This playful attitude with problem solutions ("What is another way I can express my answer?") is one that we tried hard to foster. We wanted children to view answers not as ending points but as starting places for further explorations. (3) Lauren generated new insights about measurement, division, and rounding; she discovered that even though the two areas differed slightly in the number of water drops used, the number of spoonfuls was about the same. As she talked to us afterward, she could see that a more precise measure, such as water drops, gave a finer comparison, an important insight about the potential and limits of various measuring tools. Lauren also gained some insight into converting one measure into another. Once she had determined that one spoonful contained 70 drops,

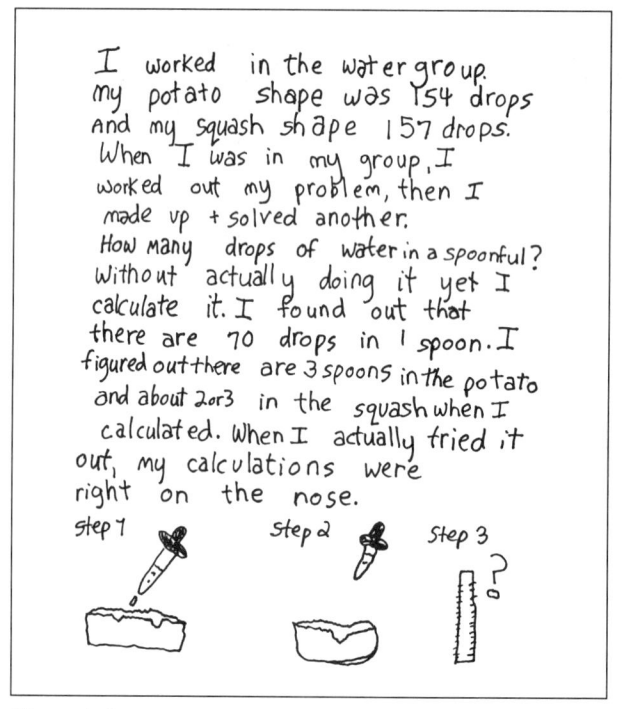

> I worked in the water group. My potato shape was 154 drops and my squash shape 157 drops. When I was in my group, I worked out my problem, then I made up + solved another.
> How many drops of water in a spoonful? Without actually doing it yet I calculate it. I found out that there are 70 drops in 1 spoon. I figured out there are 3 spoons in the potato and about 2 or 3 in the squash when I calculated. When I actually tried it out, my calculations were right on the nose.
> step 1   step 2   step 3

Figure 4–6

she knew she had to divide to determine the number of spoonfuls, but was not sure how. She used a calculator and divided 154 drops by 70 and found the answer to be 2.2, and rounded that to 3. For the other shape she divided the other way: 70 drops divided by 157 drops = .45, which she rounded to 5. (She was used to rounding to whole numbers, so she changed the decimal point of .45 to the more familiar 4.5, and then rounded to 5.) Neither answer seemed to make sense to her. David W. turned the problem back to her by suggesting that she use the strategy of mental computation: "Let's see what we get if we just try to figure it out in our head." Although it is important that calculators be available for use in the classroom, these tools do not do the thinking for children; they only do the work that we ask them to do. Lauren had used the calculator to obtain some numerical results, but she did not know which answer seemed more appropriate. As she and David W. worked together, she thought, "70 and 70 is 140, with 17 drops left." At first she thought 17 drops might be equivalent to another spoonful or two, but when David W. asked her to compare it to 70 she realized, "That's not very much of another spoonful." Although her journal entry states three spoonfuls, she realized later it was closer to two. She filled each shape with two spoonfuls and found her calculations were "right on the nose," filling each cup almost to the top with two spoonfuls each.

Using Clay to Determine Area

There were several interesting investigations involving clay. Derek filled each of his two shapes with clay and then pressed a base 10 flat on top of the clay, leaving a gridded impression that he could use to calculate the area of each shape (Figure 4–7). He obviously knew one shape was larger than the other, but he was interested in comparing two distinctly different shapes. (Also, the grid lines in his journal entry are meant as a sketch, not an exact representation.) He liked using clay because it filled the edges, but he found that the squares were cut off along the edges. He devised a unique solution that he described in his journal: "One side of the little one was too little for a block so I twisted the clay and made it into a square." He recombined pieces of the partial squares into full squares by pushing the little bits of clay together. Thus, he took advantage of the continuous property of the clay to help him calculate the area.

Michael used clay in another way (Figure 4–8). He filled the area of each of his shapes with clay and then measured each mass. His results confirmed what others had been finding: a circle yielded the largest area for a fixed perimeter. Chris F. found similar results when he weighed his clay (Figure 4–9). He had been careful to make his clay shapes the same thickness so that the comparison would be fair. However, he still wondered, "If I put more clay in one will it make a difference?" Chris wanted to calculate the difference between the two weights by piling more clay on top of shape B to see how much more he needed to add until both sides were equivalent. He investigated this idea later on. Here again a student used the results of his first exploration as a basis for posing an additional question to pursue.

> I did the clay as a stamp. I fond out that the big one was 61 cubs and the little one 17 cubs. One side of the little one was to little for a block so I twisted the clay and made it in to a scuar.
>
> Derek

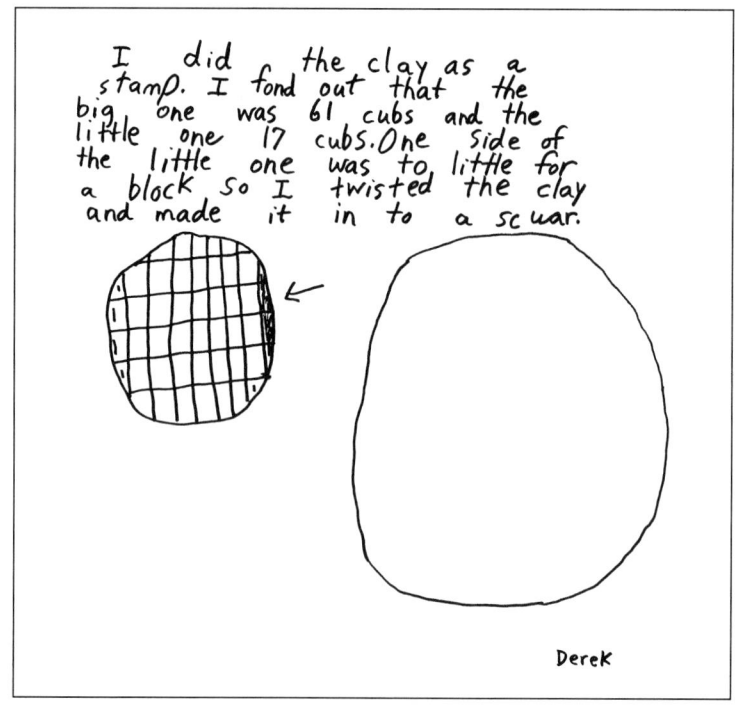

Figure 4–7

Mathematical inquirers never stand still. We later shared Chris' efforts with the class as another example of using answers to extend an investigation.

Derek went beyond his initial investigation as well. He was intrigued with the fact that the circle yielded the greatest possible area for a fixed perimeter. He traced around a jar lid to examine a circle in more detail (Figure 4–10) and confirmed for himself that all diameters are the same length. Keeping this particular attribute of circles in mind, he then challenged himself to draw a circle freehand. He measured the diameters of this shape to see how close he was and found that they were not quite equivalent (9.6, 11.8, 11.0, 9.5, 9.0). He wondered if any hand-traced circle could have "exact measurements" (i.e., all diameters the same length).

An important prerequisite for building a community that poses questions and extends investigations is the ability to look closely. Lauren looked closely at her answer of water drops and wanted to express it again using spoonfuls. Chris F. noticed that there was a difference in weight between his two shapes and decided to challenge himself with making the smaller weight equivalent to the larger one. Finally, Derek observed that circles all have equivalent diameters, and he wanted to do some further measuring with jar lids and hand-traced circles. In all these cases it is the close observation of the present circumstance—that is, drops of water, difference in weight, and equal diameters—that provides the seed for the

Using Clay to Determine Area 73

> Frist my teacher gave me some clay and I had to weigh it in a spicle way. I made two shape one was a circle and one was a sqash shape. I was tring to find out how much run around space there is in the shape. So I took some clay and made my shapes and weigh them. My Circle weigh the most at 110 g. and my sqash at 86 g. So the circle has more place to run around in.
>
> Michael

Figure 4–8

next step. Observations are attributes of a given problem situation. Once children describe some attributes, they have some particulars for extending. For instance, Derek's observation about the diameters of circles could have gone in many different directions. If we list each attribute of his observation separately we can see many possibilities:

Observations/Attributes

1. The shape is a circle.

2. The lines are diameters.

3. All diameters are equal.

4. All diameters meet in the center of the circle.

Extensions

1. What if we measured the diameters of different-sized circles?

2. If we drew other kinds of lines inside a circle, what would we find?

3. If we measured the diagonals of other polygons, would they be equivalent?

4. What if we tried to find the center of other regular polygons? Is this possible?

> I put clay in each shap and the tin foil was the shap and I put it on the skal and A was more, it was 67 and B was 29. I still wonder if I put more clay in one will it make a deverens.
>
> shaps
>
> A
>
> B

Figure 4–9

As described in earlier chapters, this was the kind of investigative mind-set that we wanted to permeate our classroom community. In the context of this present exploration of inventing tools to calculate area, some different directions did arise. We shared these ideas with the class so that everyone had more examples to draw from as they thought about their own extensions.

However, sometimes children's previous instructional background prevented them from adopting these norms of invention and extension. For instance, Kelvin measured across and down each of his shapes and then multiplied each pair of numbers together to obtain the area. Robin asked him, "Why did you do that?" "That's what we learned last year. Just multiply these two together," he replied. "But why would that make sense to you?" Robin asked. "I don't know. That's just what we were told to do." In fourth grade Kelvin had been given some rules to follow on how to calculate area. Although he obtained mostly right answers the previous year, his comments to Robin clearly demonstrate that right answers are not synonymous with understanding. Even worse, getting right answers but not

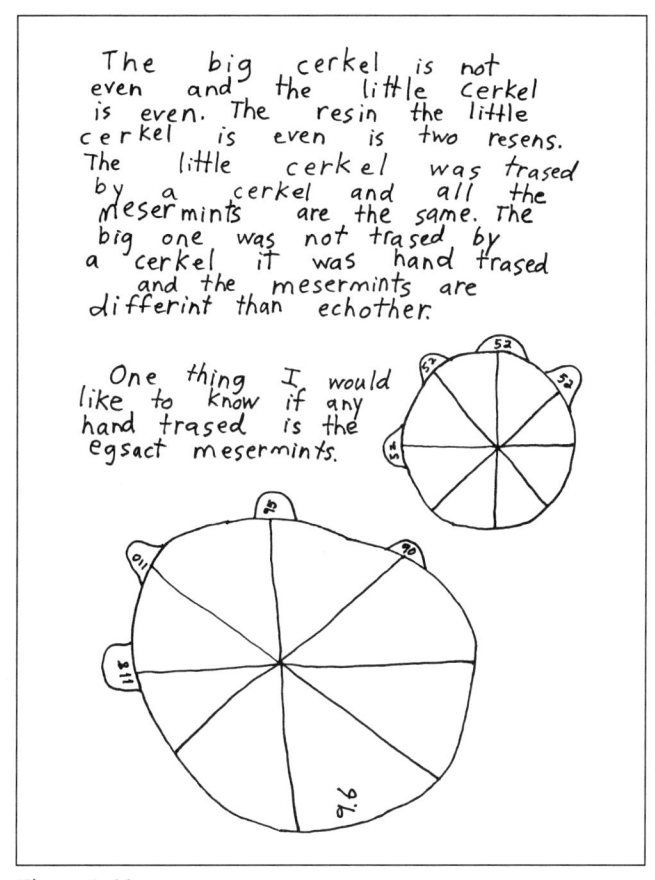

> The big cerkel is not even and the little cerkel is even. The resin the little cerkel is even is two resens. The little cerkel was trased by a cerkel and all the mesermints are the same. The big one was not trased by a cerkel it was hand trased and the mesermints are differint than echother.
>
> One thing I would like to know if any hand trased is the egsact mesermints.

Figure 4–10

knowing why strips learners of their most precious gift—the ability to make sense of problem situations. As a disempowered learner who was following someone else's rules, Kelvin was obviously not one who dared to invent a strategy or extend an investigation. He had been trained to be a more passive learner, waiting for the teacher to show him the way.

So how do we deal with students who enter with this dysfunctional attitude toward learning? We continue to have peers share their inventions and discoveries so that we make public the process of constructing one's own knowledge. We continue to ask them to explain their thinking, both orally and in journals. We often use the question, "Why would that make sense to you?" so that he begins to assume ownership for the sense making. We have also learned that each child is different. Some children hold on to memorized rules and procedures longer than others, comfortable in following what others have told them to do. In contrast, other children who have had a similar instructional past find these new norms about learning less threatening, and are more eager to let go of previous inhibitions. We do the best we can to draw out each child's voice and emphasize that the theme of our discussions is thinking, not regurgitation. We want to emphasize process over product and sense over symbols. This is not to say that products and symbols are not important; they are critical. However, we want to be sure that children can understand and make sense of what they are learning.

Summarizing Our Findings

As we reflected on this experience, we felt that the children had made some important insights about measuring and tools. They learned that they could compare the areas of two shapes by inventing a variety of strategies; they saw the advantage of continuous materials to fill in the contours of irregular shapes; they noted the importance of counting partial squares to obtain a more accurate calculation when using a square measure; they realized that measurements are not really exact, but only our best estimates; they saw that some tools (such as a scale) were more accurate than others (such as pencil lead); and they experienced mathematics as a field for invention and exploration. The children used some of these understandings later in the year when they took a field trip to Charleston. They learned about a round house that was built along the coast after Hurricane Hugo; it not only provided maximum space for a fixed perimeter but also demonstrated a more aerodynamically round shape to withstand high winds. They also discovered that long ago Charleston had property tax that was based on how much footage faced the road. To avoid paying high taxes, residents built long rectangular houses, minimizing the amount of land that abutted the roadway. The children saw that sometimes even tax codes can influence the perimeter and shape of a town's architecture.

As the children reflected on this experience, they kept confirming that the circle yielded the greatest area:

NEAL: I discovered that a rounded shape weighs more than a raindrop shape. The roundest shape weighed more.

ERIN: I figured out that the circle was heavier than the egg roll . . . more units fitted in there.

BRANDI: I found out that the circle is the biggest. The circle has more space inside. The square is second. I learned that string can make all kinds of shapes and sizes. People can also live in all shapes and sizes.

BRANDON: My circle was bigger than the square or the rectangle. It was more wider than the others. My circle won because for one thing I wanted it to win, and another thing it weighed more.

Since we wanted to encourage the open-ended nature of inquiry, we asked the children to record other wonders they wished to pursue:

CRYSTAL: I would like to do it again but use different items for measuring.

COLE: I wonder if we could use bigger objects (for calculating area).

KELVIN: I want to know which is bigger, a circle or a hexagon.

CHRIS B.: I would like to try this again but use a longer string.

LAUREN: I would like to find out the smallest shape you can make without overlapping the strings. I would also like to have a smaller string and see the largest shape you could make.

We tried to make raising these "wonders" a regular routine after any math investigation. Sometimes Robin devoted additional class time for these follow-up investigations. At other times she used these wonders as homework assignments, or posted them on a chart in the room for children to pursue during math workshop time (see Chapter 6). We wanted the children to witness the spiraling nature of inquiry learning; that is, the more they observed and discovered, the more they could extend and question.

The class also had numerous explanations for how a fixed perimeter can yield an assortment of areas:

DAVID G.: I think that the string stretched out is going to have more room because it's a bigger area (REALLY WEIRD).

TALITHA: When you make different shapes out of the same length string they look different but they should have the same amount of space to run around in. I think that even if it's a different shape that if you use all of the same length string all of them should have the same space to run around in.

GREG: It was weird that everybody had the same size string and had longer shape[s] [i.e., different areas]. Everybody had large shape[s]. Some people had weird shape[s].

For some of the children, such as Talitha and Greg, the relationship between area and perimeter still remained a bit mysterious. Although they knew that the circle yielded the largest possible area for a fixed perimeter, they realized that it was not always easy to tell which shape was the largest. As teachers we knew we could not legislate understanding; learners must create it for themselves. However, the children's lingering doubts and questions provided valuable assessment information, and were helpful in planning further curricular experiences.

Going Beyond the Experience

1. Challenge children to use the geoboard to investigate further the relationship between perimeter and area. Ask children to create figures, using only horizontal and vertical lines, with an area of 5 square units. What do they notice about the perimeters? Or the

children might work with a fixed perimeter of 12 units and observe what happens to the area.

2. Pose questions that encourage children to create other tools for measuring. For instance: How could we measure time (often leading to sundials and water clocks)? How could we measure the length of the classroom (books, body lengths)?

3. Invite children to estimate and calculate the area of many irregular shapes, such as leaves or the petals of flowers. An example of a botanist who makes these leaf-area calculations as part of an ecological study can be found in *The Most Beautiful Roof in the World: Exploring the Rainforest Canopy* (Lasky 1997).

4. Challenge children to calculate the surface area of different parts of their bodies, such as feet, hands, arms, and legs. Such calculations can help children understand the human body's regulation of temperature. Children might also study how plants and animals, such as a desert cactus, use surface areas to survive.

5. Investigate how marketing people use area and volume to sell their products. How are shapes of certain containers made to look larger, even though the surface areas of several containers are the same?

6. Ask children to investigate the area of their classroom. How does it compare to the areas of other classrooms? Are larger classrooms given to the largest classes? Can the children recommend changes to the principal?

7. Connect these ideas to social studies by examining the different factors that influenced the architectural style of a given culture (or area in the neighborhood). These factors might include availability of resources, climate, or family roles and traditions.

8. Invite an architect to class to discuss the decisions that she makes in utilizing interior and exterior spaces.

5 Mathematicians Discover Patterns and Relationships

Creating patterns is what mathematicians do best (Schoenfeld 1994). As they solve problems, mathematicians seek out patterns of regularity and logical order. They do not simply describe a pattern and stop, but ask questions about those patterns: How do we know a pattern when we see one? What constitutes a pattern? Why is it occurring? How can we represent it? How might we modify or extend it? These are exploratory, tentative questions. For this reason a search for patterns must occur in a supportive community. In this chapter you will see children engaged in a geometry experience in which they discover several interesting patterns. We describe our attempts at building a sense of community and shared vulnerability among our students. We encouraged the children to take risks to share provisional theories about how those patterns worked and to represent their findings in various ways. We supported children in questioning and debating the theories of others so that they took an active role in constructing their own understanding. We also summarized key points of conversations so all children could reflect on the current set of ideas. We asked children to reflect on the nature of their conversations so that they could become more aware of the power of talk in a collaborative community. Last, we teachers realized in a more profound way that we, too, were inquirers in this classroom. We realized anew that we did not know all the answers to the mathematical questions that arose. We found that teaching for understanding means exposing our own vulnerability, but it also means legitimizing our place in the very community we are striving to create.

The Initial Investigation

We wanted to build on the previous experiences that the children had with circles and perimeter/area. We therefore chose another experience that highlighted the functional use of geometry. It placed children in the role of structural engineers, as they examined properties of shapes that would strengthen their building designs. The experience took place during three one-hour class sessions and comprised three main activities:

1. a hands-on investigation to explore the strength of triangles
2. a discussion of the patterns that the children found in the data
3. an application of this knowledge through the building of their own structures

These activities also incorporated patterns and basic functional relationships as well as work with regular polygons and three-dimensional shapes. All of these goals were part of the fifth-grade curriculum. However, we felt that this experience addressed these goals in a more integrated way by embedding them in a meaningful context. The specific task that we gave the children is described in the box on the next page.

As we discussed this investigation we felt that it offered not only rich mathematical opportunities but also potential benefits to the growth of the classroom community. These benefits are outlined in the lesson plan chart.

As the children built the shapes, they wrote about and drew the patterns that they found in their journals. A look at their journals reveals the variety of their observations. A summary of their findings is included the table on page 83, Children's Findings About Polygons.

Hedda's writing nicely conveyed the movement characteristics of each shape: the triangle was "sturdy," the square was "not so sturdy" or "kind of loose," and the five-sided shape she called "very loose." Through her descriptive language Hedda identified a progressive pattern of rigidity and looseness as figures increased in their number of sides.

Derek and Neal focused on the pattern of an increasing number of struts. Derek wrote: "I noticed that the bigger the shape the more strips it takes to make it not move." Neal found these same patterns but described it in his own way: "What I found out was a pattern. See the first one [triangle] had no struts. The second one [square] it had one strut. So if you add one more line to it, it would take one more strut. I also found out the triangle could fit in all the shapes" (i.e., the struts created triangular regions inside each polygon).

Chris B. organized his findings in another way by showing the increasing pattern of struts through his drawings (Figure 5–1). He methodically listed each shape, showing what it looked like before and after the struts were attached, and gave a written commentary about why more and more struts were needed. He concluded: "The struts reinforce the sides so that the shape will not bend as easily." Brandi conveyed the patterns she saw in yet another way. She did not use any drawings but wrote a narrative that summarized her major findings: "Today in math we made shapes. We made some shapes 3–8 [sided]. After we made the shapes we had to make it so it wouldn't move. It was fun and sometimes it was hard. In all of my shapes I can see a triangle. They're not the same triangle. On the 4's I had 2 triangles. On the 5's I had 3 triangles. On the 6's I had 4 triangles. I noticed that every shape had one more triangle. We put struts in the shapes. We had to make them like the triangle. The struts helped it stay in place." Brandi made some important observations: (1) Since the triangle was the most stable

Investigating the Strength of Regular Polygons

The Challenge

Students are given strips cut from card stock. Each strip has a hole punched close to either end. Children build a series of regular polygons from three-sided to eight-sided, fastening the sides together with brads. The children soon notice that only the triangle remains rigid; the sides of the other shapes flop around and collapse. The challenge is to make these other shapes rigid so that their sides do *not* collapse. The children can attach additional struts, or supports, to accomplish this task. These struts have holes punched in one end, and as the children add them to the figure, they cut off the leftover portion and punch the second end to secure it to the polygon. There are several rules for adding struts:

- The struts must go from vertex to vertex (not vertex to side, or side to side). For instance, this attachment is allowed:

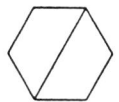

This attachment is *not* allowed:

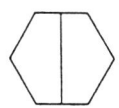

- The struts must not cross each other (which forces children to be efficient in the number of struts they use).
- The polygon must retain its original number of sides.
- Use the fewest number of struts to make the polygon rigid.

Materials

1. 25 strips, 1 cm × 7 cm, with holes punched close to both ends
2. 10 strips, 1 cm × 30 cm, with holes punched at one end
3. 25 brads (½")
4. Paper punches (one per two students)
5. Scissors

Lesson Plan and Intended Outcomes

Lesson Plan	Intended Outcomes—Process	Intended Outcomes—Product
Challenge children to attach struts to polygons to make them rigid. (45 minutes)	Children discover several different ways to solve the problem.	Children use models to represent geometric relationships.
Conduct a class discussion of the findings. (15 minutes)	Children share difficulties and problems as well as insights and relationships. They note patterns in the results.	Children compare properties of regular polygons.
Lead a more in-depth discussion of the function between number of sides and number of struts. (20 minutes)	Children explain and justify the patterns in different ways. They challenge each other's ideas and revise their thinking.	Children use patterns to construct generalizations.
Ask children to reflect on the conversation and the different theories proposed. (10 minutes)	Children express their current thinking in words, pictures, and writing.	Children interpret data both orally and in writing.
Invite children to use their knowledge of two-dimensional shapes to build the strongest or tallest three-dimensional structure they could. (40 minutes)	Children take risks as they test out different structures. They share their revisions in the design of these structures.	Children compare and contrast two- and three-dimensional shapes.
Ask children to reflect on their problem-solving strategies as they work with a partner. (10 minutes)	Children recognize the benefits and potential problems of trying to work together.	Children identify problem-solving strategies.
Encourage children to read books that examine the building ideas of others. (30 minutes)	Children connect mathematical principles of design to other buildings in the world.	Children apply geometric concepts to real-world applications.

Mathematicians Discover Patterns and Relationships 83

Children's Findings About Polygons

Number of Sides of Polygon	Number of Struts Needed to Make It Rigid	Number of Triangles Formed Inside
3	0	1
4	1	2
5	2	3
6	3	4
7	4	5
8	5	6

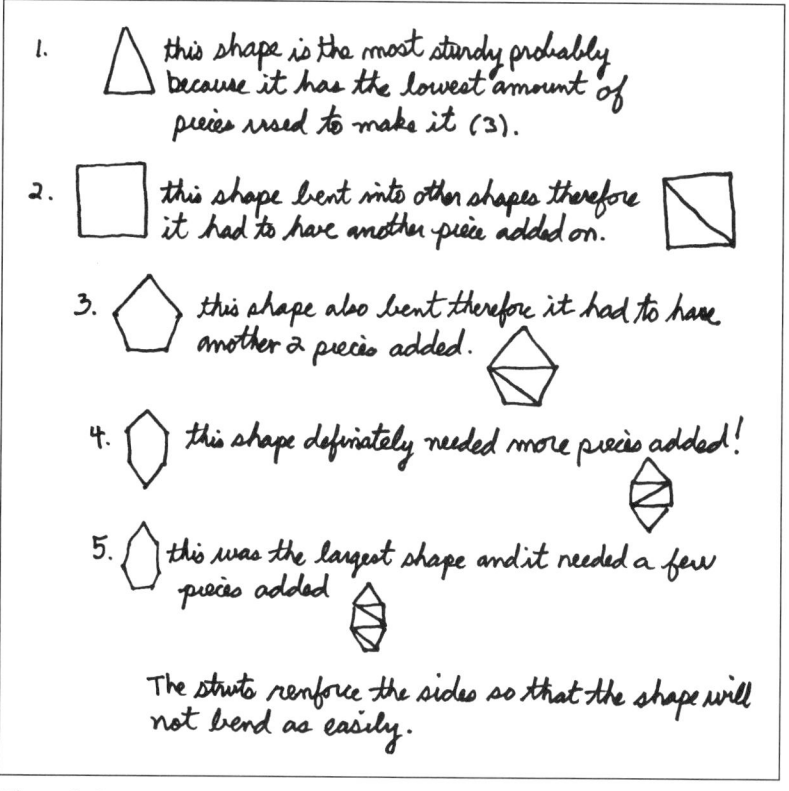

1. △ this shape is the most sturdy probably because it has the lowest amount of pieces used to make it (3).

2. ▢ this shape bent into other shapes therefore it had to have another piece added on. ◳

3. ⬠ this shape also bent therefore it had to have another 2 pieces added.

4. ⬡ this shape definitely needed more pieces added!

5. ⬯ this was the largest shape and it needed a few pieces added

The struts reinforce the sides so that the shape will not bend as easily.

Figure 5–1

shape, the interior region of each polygon was subdivided into other triangles to make that shape rigid; (2) every shape was divided into triangles; (3) the interior triangles were not all the same size; and (4) as the number of sides of the polygon increased by one so the number of triangles formed also increased by one.

Other students were more succinct in describing the patterns they saw and more willing to predict how those patterns might continue. David G. wrote: "Today we worked with architecture. There are three less struts than sides for every object. It was fun!" Latching on to patterns is part of what mathematicians do, and David G. was feeling that excitement for himself. Other children made predictions as well. Lauren completed figures with three to six sides and wondered if this pattern would continue (Figure 5–2). She made a visual and a numerical record of the pattern she saw, predicted that the sequence might continue, and then urged herself to "check this out." Lauren was doing what mathematicians do by not only noting patterns but also predicting how they might continue, and gathering more data to confirm that prediction. Bobby wrote, "Today we did building. All them have a triangle in it. I wonder what would 10 look like." He began to draw the number of struts needed to make a ten-sided figure rigid. Thus, his wondering prompted him to create a natural extension to this initial investigation. Jennifer noted the difference of two between the number of sides and the number of triangles and predicted that pattern would also continue: "I think there is a pattern like 3 – 1, 4 – 2, 5 – 3, 6 – 4, 7 – 5, 8 – 6, 9 – 7. I think my prediction is right if not all the corners had to be out like [a rectangle]. I wish [we were permitted to collapse shapes into rectangles] but it has to be like this [a hexagon]."

The First Conversation: Mathematicians Analyze Patterns and Develop Theories

As the children shared their individual results, we recorded their findings on the board for us all to examine. Some children had investigated all polygons having

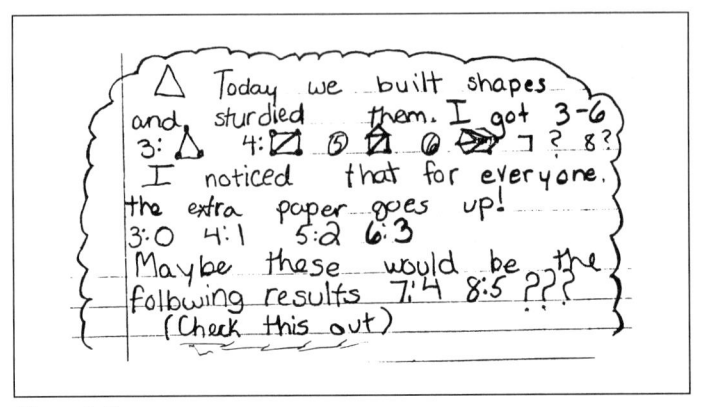

Figure 5–2

from three to eight sides, while others did not get any further than the hexagon. Summarizing all the data for the class to consider consolidated the group's findings and gave everyone the opportunity to examine the data in detail. (See the earlier table, Children's Findings About Polygons.) The chart helped to highlight some of the patterns that individual children had discovered (e.g., the number of struts is three less than the number of sides, and the number of triangles formed is two less than the number of sides). In drawing some of their discoveries on the board the children found several solutions for each shape, such as the hexagon:

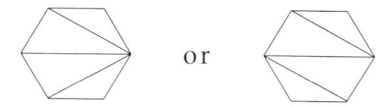

Although the placement of the struts was different, the total number of struts used was still the same. The children noticed that one solution showed all struts emanating from the same vertex while the other solution showed a zigzag pattern. As mathematicians the children were detecting not only numerical patterns in the chart but also visual patterns in their drawings. We were realizing that a supportive mathematical community encourages learners to express what they have discovered in different ways, such as charts and drawings. In this way children generate new views of the data and new ideas for the group to consider.

David noticed a special feature of the five-sided polygon: "In the five-sided shape there is a square and a triangle, and those are the first two shapes I just made."

Melanie saw another interesting feature: "On the five-sided there's three triangles and two stripes [struts], and three and two is five."

"Does that pattern work for any of the other shapes?" we teachers asked. We found that it did not, but wondered later, "What is unique about five that makes it the only case? How close do the other figures get to reaching this equivalence?" As learners we made our own chart. We found that the total was always an odd number, increasing by two each time.

Sides	Triangles	Struts		
5	3	2	3 + 2 = 5	even
6	4	3	4 + 3 = 7	1 more
7	5	4	5 + 4 = 9	2 more
8	6	5	6 + 5 = 11	3 more

We find, as we continue to encourage children to share their observations, that we too are challenged to pursue new patterns and relationships. If we, as teachers, are pushed intellectually, then we know a spirit of inquiry has been established. We are then truly co-equals with our students (Woodward and Serebrin, 1989), both contributing mutually valued resources to the present task. A sense of community develops when students are teachers and teachers are learners.

As the children discussed the results further, they hypothesized about the number of struts for an even larger figure. The following excerpts from that discussion demonstrate the variety of theories that the children proposed as well as the role of language in supporting their exploration.

DAVID G.: There's always 3 less struts than there are sides.

TEACHER: Tell them about the theory you wrote in your journal.

DAVID G.: Since there's 3 less struts for each shape, then I think there would be— Like, if you have 369 sides you might have 123 struts, because you divide it by 3 . . . [369 ÷ 3 = 123; seems dissatisfied with answer]. I don't know. I keep changing my theory.

TEACHER: I know. Well, let's talk about this. We've noticed that we're always 3 less struts than the number of sides for polygons with 4 to 8 sides. So, David's theory was, if I had a figure of 369 sides, how many struts would I use? He suggested maybe to divide by 3. He's not sure if that's right or not. What do you think?

DAVID G.: I think maybe divide by 2.

TEACHER: So if you had a 100-sided figure—

DAVID G.: You'd have 50 struts.

TEACHER: Does someone have another idea?

David G. took a risk to share his tentative thinking. Laying bare one's rough-draft thinking can happen only in a supportive community that respects being uncertain as an important mathematical disposition. We have found that to build a classroom community it must be clear from the very start that the *idea* is being laid out for consideration, *not* the individual. Thinking is the currency of the conversation (Hiebert 1997). It is interesting to note that David G. was the first person to speak after the teacher summarized the issue. The teacher's rephrasing of his thinking gave him time to mull over his ideas further and return with a revised theory. Both David G. and the teacher addressed the idea of generalization by considering shapes with many more sides. The relationship between the number of sides and the number of struts is a functional relationship. One of the powerful benefits of a function is that it allows learners to predict. So the question they raised was an important one. How could we determine the number of struts needed to make a shape rigid that has 369 sides, or 100 sides? Patterns are the first bits of evidence a mathematician needs to identify a function and build a generalization. Involving children in developing these generalizations gives them the thrill of creating a mathematician's favorite labor-saving device: "Look, I know what the answer is going to be, and I don't even have to test it out!" The conversation continued:

COLE: I think you probably have 97 (number of struts for a 100-sided figure).

TEACHER: Why?

COLE: Because there's always 3 less struts than the number of sides.

TEACHER: OK. Let's go back to David for a minute. What was your thinking when you said divide by 2?

DAVID G.: With 6 sides you have 3 struts, so 6 divided by 2 is 3. And 4 sides divided by 1 strut is . . . no. Certain numbers . . . certain even numbers can be divided to equal the struts. Like $4 \div 4 = 1$, $6 \div 2 = 3$, um . . .

TEACHER: So you were looking for some kind of pattern.

LAUREN: Maybe it has something to do with certain even numbers.

DAVID G.: Whatever you can divide the number into, I think. If you put 5 into 100, that's 20 times. And there's 2 struts in each 5, so there ought to be a total of 40 struts.

TEACHER: He's revised his theory. Now he thinks it's 40 struts. What do people think of that idea, or does someone have another idea about the number of struts for a 100-sided figure?

Cole disagreed with David G., arguing that there ought to be three fewer struts than the number of sides. The teacher then returned to David G. so he could explain his thinking.

As we teachers analyzed these conversations together, we realized that this emphasis on making one's thinking visible is a key tenet in the fields of reading and writing instruction as well. Just as we want children to explain their authoring decisions in their personal narrative writing, so too we want them to explain their decisions as mathematical thinkers (Mills, O'Keefe, and Whitin 1996). David G. continued to look for some relationship to describe the pattern and persisted in using division to explain the relationship. He developed a ratio, which is a particular kind of pattern, to justify his answer. If there are 2 struts for a 5-sided shape, and there are 20 fives in 100, then 20 × 2 would be 40 struts for a 100-sided figure. The teacher acknowledged David G.'s right to revise ("He's revised his theory") so that others would recognize its legitimate place in class discussions. The debate continued:

RICHIE: I think it's 97, because it's minus 3 on the other shapes.

COLE: He said it's half, right [6 sides divided in half = 3 struts]?

TEACHER: Yes.

COLE: But look at 4. That's not half [4 has only 1 strut, not 2]. Does that mean if it's 10, it should be 5 struts?

TEACHER: According to his theory, yes.

COLE: But I think it's just 3 less.

TEACHER: Someone say some more about this whole business . . .

BRANDI: It think it's 3 less, because on the 8 it's 3 less, and 7 it's 3 less.

Cole continued to dispute David G.'s theory and mustered some evidence to prove his point: If David is dividing the number of sides in half to determine the number of struts, his theory does not work for a four-sided shape or a ten-sided shape. However, what disturbed us about this part of the conversation is that we did not direct Cole's questions to David G. but we answered them ourselves. We realized that we do not want every question or comment filtered through the teacher. That is why we use the collective nouns of "we" and "us" rather than "me" as we discuss ideas, as in "Who has another idea to share with *us*?" In hindsight, we could have said to Cole, "Ask David if that is what he meant." This response builds more of a sense of community because children can then discuss ideas directly with the authors of those ideas. Otherwise, teachers are put in the awkward position of trying to interpret what another child intended. If we truly believe that thinking ought to be the focus of class conversations, then we must allow the thinkers to converse directly with each other.

As the discussion continued there was more debate about the number of struts for a many-sided polygon:

TEACHER: Let's go back to David again, since he's the person who stirred up this conversation.

DAVID G.: I think maybe what you do is subtract 3 off of each number. Like, 5,637 you might have 2,304 struts. (He subtracts 5,637 − 3,333 = 2,304; he is attracted to the "less 3 theory" and applies it to a larger number in this way.)

TEACHER: So you agree with subtracting 3, but you think you ought to subtract 3 from every number. This is a new theory. Who would like to talk about this theory, or another one? This is a great conversation.

LESLIE: I still think it's take away 3, so it would be 5,634.

TEACHER: Why wouldn't you take away 3 from all the numbers?

LESLIE: (long pause) I don't know.

TEACHER: David, why did you subtract 3 from every number? What was your rationale for that?

DAVID G.: Well, see, when you get a high number, such as 5,637, it would be kind of strange to just subtract 3, instead of 3,333.

CRYSTAL: When you had 4 sides and 1 strut, you only took away 3. But when you have 5,637, you're taking away a thousand, and some other stuff, so you're taking away too much.

DEREK: If you take away 3 from every number, then if you do that for 100, it wouldn't be 97, it would be some other number . . .

TEACHER: Yes, David, with your theory, how would we take away 3 from every number if we had 100 sides?

DAVID G.: You should only take away 33 (not 333). So it would be 67 struts.

COLE: David, you keep changing your hypothesis about everything. It sounds like you're really not sure about which one it is.

DAVID G.: Every time somebody else says something it gives [me] some other idea that one [theory] might be wrong, but this other one might be right . . .

BRANDON: I don't understand the whole . . . all right, this is what I heard. When you have a large amount of sides, some people say it's 3 less. I don't understand that because why can't there be the same amount of struts as the sides? I don't understand.

(We look at his figures and note 4 sides = 1 strut, 5 sides = 2 struts, etc.)

TEACHER: So you're asking if it's ever possible to have the same number of struts as sides. Maybe someone can answer that.

BRANDI: I want to know how we're going to know which one is right?

TEACHER: That's probably what I'd ask you.

JENNIFER: Make it [i.e., a 100-sided polygon].

TEACHER: Yes, one way is to make a 100-sided figure. Maybe there is a simpler way . . .

DAVID G.: For that problem of 100 sides, there should be 70 struts in a 100 because if there's 5 struts in 8 sides, then there would be 6 struts for 9 sides, and then 7 struts for 10 sides. So if you just multiply 10 by 10 you get 100, and if you multiply 7 by 10 you get 70.

DEREK: There could be a couple of different ways. I mean, maybe one answer is not the right one.

LAUREN: I think it's 97 and I think I've got it proven. If we were right about going up one each time, and I went up all the way to 100, and I got 97 [displays large chart of her numbers].

TEACHER: Lauren continued our chart as a way to prove that a 100-sided shape would have 97 struts.

TEACHER (ROBIN): I was just looking at Brandi's 8-sided figure, and was thinking, if you start at one corner, you don't go to the corner next to it (in either direction) because that's a side, so you go to the next one. So you skip an angle here and go to the next one. And so you skipped 2 angles, and the one you started with doesn't really count. So does that work for everything?

(Robin drew the following figure on the board.)

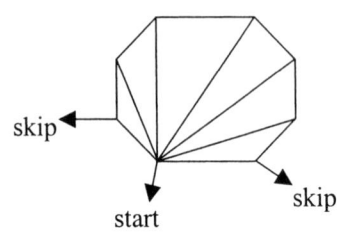

TEACHER: That's a good idea. Let me summarize what we've been saying. How are we going to find out the number of struts needed to make a 100-sided figure rigid? First, we could follow Lauren's way and make a table. Second, we could try to make it, but that may be fairly difficult. Third, we could try to create a theory, like what Ms. Cox did, based on her observations of the figures and then her deductions about those observations. Fourth, we could draw it, and try to figure it out that way. Any other ideas on how we could test out our problem?

COLE: If you just draw it, you can't hold it or move it. So you really couldn't test it.

TEACHER: Yes, you're right. We couldn't test it with our hands.

MELANIE: Maybe for 100, we could do 50, do a half, and then add those two up together.

CHRIS: I don't agree with Melanie, because if you make it into two 50's, that would come out different than a 100-sided shape.

David G. continued to offer other ideas, which some disagreed with and others used to develop their own theories (such as the concept of a ratio that Melanie used). We wondered later if we had allowed David G. to dominate the conversation. In fact, we did keep returning the conversation to him as other children responded to his current theory. Part of the reason we continued to solicit his ideas was that we felt his willingness to be such a risk taker and share his tentative thinking was an important stance for the class to witness.

Another reason was that we knew David G., and he was not one who would often take a leading role in class conversations. However, this experience ignited his imagination, and we wanted to allow him the time to be the catalyst for this conversation. David G. was also the one who kept offering alternative theories. We felt that his different interpretations would cause others to rethink their own ideas about the generalizability of this pattern.

Teachers Are Vulnerable Too: Reflecting on What We Did Not Know

This conversation helped show how vulnerable we were as teachers in a collaborative, investigative community. Although most children continued to argue that a 100-sided figure ought to have 97 struts, there were others who constructed alternative theories using the ratio as the basis of their calculations. Some refuted this idea of a ratio by claiming that it did not work with the numbers that they had tabulated so far—that is, a 4-sided shape has 1 strut, so an 8-sided shape ought to yield 2 struts (given this ratio of 4:1), but it has 5 struts. This reasoning was a logical rebuttal. However, we must honestly admit that we did not know enough about the mathematics to figure out how to clarify the distinction between a ratio and a function. We felt that both were patterns but wondered what made them patterns. Were they patterns because they described predictable relationships? What is the definition of a pattern? How is a ratio different from a function? Why did David G.'s (and others') reasoning about a ratio to determine the number of struts not work? These were questions that we posed for ourselves weeks later, after listening again to this taped conversation. In talking to a university colleague, we found answers to some of these questions (see notes at the end of this chapter).

As we reflected further on this conversation, we were struck again by the fact that, as Heaton said, "All participants need to expect to learn from one another" (2000, p. 150). It is not that teachers do not prepare lessons in advance or have ideas on how to extend that experience. Rather, the point is that when we enter classrooms curious about how our students make sense of problem situations, we must also enter with the mind-set "expecting that what we learn about our students' understandings may reshape how *we* see things, raise new questions about what it is that *we* think they understand, reshape the purposes of whatever it is *we* thought they were doing . . ." (p. 151). We as teachers must also honestly admit that when we teach for understanding, there are going to be questions for which we do not know the answers. In this investigation, we were learning that we needed to openly question our own mathematical understandings. Heaton states again: "It is not the students' responsibility to match their understandings with the teacher's. It is the teacher's responsibility to push him- or herself to make sense of what it is that students understand" (p. 159). In this sense we are being the very inquirers that we want our students to be: sharing what we do not know, being uncertain of how to proceed, questioning our own understandings, being reflective about our instructional decisions. Such honesty is risky business. David W. wondered whether he might be perceived differently by Robin for not having thought through the finer distinctions between a ratio and a function. Wasn't he the "university expert?" How did it look for him to fumble around and not know what to do next? He wondered if it would have been easier to gloss over this issue, move on to the next part of the activity, and not bother to look closely at what the children were trying to make sense of. Such reflections can be embarrassing and discomforting, but also enlightening. David W. realized even more that his role as a university collaborator was actually one of a fellow inquirer.

As Robin reflected more on this conversation, she gained additional insights into the values that underpinned her classroom community. It was these values that Robin had developed in her reading and writing workshop and was now carrying over to a mathematical context. These open-ended, exploratory conversations were helping her make the transition to an inquiry-based mathematics classroom. However, by opening up the conversation in this way, Robin was also realizing that the children would be grappling with a variety of mathematical concepts and would be raising questions for which she did not know the answers. She too was now exposing her vulnerability, but she saw benefits in this stance as a learner. She had worked hard to foster an inquiry stance toward reading and writing, and she was used to having her students pose questions about scientific problems or an author's intentions for which she had no ready answers. As a fellow learner, she was used to seeking answers to these questions by conferring with other teachers at her school or the local university. Problems encountered in the area of mathematics should be no different. As an inquirer she had learned not to be threatened by not knowing. In fact, not knowing kept her growing as a professional. It is an interesting paradox that by showing this vulnerability, she was actually gaining confidence in herself as a mathematical thinker.

Conjectures About Patterns Build a Sense of Community

An important facet of this previous classroom discussion is that it is laced with tentative thinking. David G. began the discussion by sharing his hypothesis, "There's always three less struts than there are sides." Indeed, David G. played a key role in sustaining the conversation by his willingness to play around with various ideas and entertain alternative theories. When Cole questioned David G. for "changing your hypothesis about everything," David G. readily admitted the power of the social community in shaping his thinking: "Every time somebody else says something it gives [me] some other idea that one [theory] might be wrong, but this other one might be right." The ideas of others enable us to view our own thinking from new perspectives. Another important contribution that David G. made was his willingness to make his thinking "visible" (Gallas 1994), as well as share ideas that were only partially formed. His specific descriptions of his hypotheses in-process created more speculation by other students, and even generated new hypotheses of his own. Making thinking visible gives learners a new perspective for extending their own thinking.

The conversation also demonstrated the important role that disagreement has in a mathematics community. As children challenged the theories of others (particularly David G.), they sometimes caused the authors of these ideas to revise them. For instance, when Cole questioned David G.'s theories, David sometimes abandoned or revised them. Derek and Chris also questioned several proposed ideas. However, the tone of these challenges, which is not conveyed by merely reading the transcript, was not sarcastic or derogatory. Rather, children were either offering logical arguments or raising new questions for the authors of these ideas to consider. This kind of intellectual exchange must be at the heart of what a mathematics community can do for its members. It is the kind of classroom discourse and social interaction advocated in NCTM's *Principles and Standards:* "[In these communities] students propose mathematical ideas and conjectures, learn to evaluate their own thinking and that of others, and develop mathematical reasoning skills" (2000, p. 21).

This conversation also highlighted the important role of the teacher in fostering these mathematical conversations. This role features the following strategies:

1. Encourage children to make their thinking visible (Gallas 1994). It is not enough for children to offer their hypotheses; they must also be challenged to explain how they came to formulate them.

2. Keep track of the author of each idea. As new theories arise, return to the originators of these earlier ideas and ask them what they are thinking now. Ask them why they agree or disagree with some of the current ideas. The more opportunities learners have to refute, substantiate, or modify the theories of others, the more perspectives they gain on their own theories (Yackel and Cobb 1996).

3. Insist that the questions children raise are answered by the classroom community and not by the teacher alone. When Brandi asked, "How are we going to know which one is right?" we asked the class to help answer that question.

4. Periodically, summarize the main points of the conversation. In this way the children can reflect upon some of the major issues that have been raised.

5. Maintain a willingness to remain divergent. We learned this lesson from Derek, who said, "There could be a couple of different ways . . ." He was encouraging us not to shut down any possibilities and not to assume there was only a single solution. This kind of attitude is an important one for a teacher to demonstrate because it encourages learners to continue to entertain various interpretations. In fact, as we reflected on this conversation later on, we realized we could have thwarted this entire discussion by saying at the outset to David, "Yes, that's the pattern. You've got it. There are always three fewer struts than the number of sides." The purpose of mathematical conversations is not to discover the right answer and be done with it; rather, the purpose is to formulate further conjectures and generate alternative explanations. At the beginning of the conversation, David, Jake, Chris, and Cole were all quite adamant about the theory of three fewer struts than sides. However, as David began to create other theories, these other children also began to waiver in their support of their initial theory. They might have been influenced by their respect for David G. as a mathematical thinker as well as by the persuasiveness of his argument. Nevertheless, a spirit

of remaining divergent fostered additional hypothesizing, causing all members of the class to reconsider their current theories about how these numbers worked. Even though many did not change their initial theories, just having to reflect, analyze, and refute these other theories helped to strengthen their understandings. The conversation highlights the importance of living in a collaborative community in which learners push, extend, and challenge each other; learners can outgrow themselves only with the help of others.

Children Reflect on the Conversation

After this lengthy discussion we asked the children to record in their journals their current thinking about this numerical relationship between the number of sides and the number of struts. Journals allow all children to take a stand on issues, thereby developing an environment in which all voices are heard. We have found that reluctant speakers are sometimes more willing to read aloud from their journal. Some children become more confident as speakers and more assured of their mathematical ability when they can share their writings and drawings. As the children read aloud their reflections, many saw the pattern of three fewer struts than sides as the most convincing. They wrote:

CRYSTAL: Today we had a longggggg discussion about different people's theories on the sides and struts. I like the theory to just take three away because I understand it.

LAUREN: I think my theory is 97 struts. I think this because I made a chart from 3 – 100. #100 read 97. I used the class theory that each time the extra paper [strut] goes up.

DEREK: I think Lauren's idea to make it because that's what we did on everything. It's like 3 – 0, 4 – 1, 5 – 2, 6 – 3, 7 – 4, 8 – 5 and so on. It would be better to see it right in front of you.

RICHIE: I think it takes 97 struts to make 100 sides because there are always 3 more sides than there are struts and the others are too complicated to understand.

BRANDI: My theory is that it's 97 because all the others are 3 away. I also think there is 97 struts in 100 because Ms. Cox said that you skip, like this:

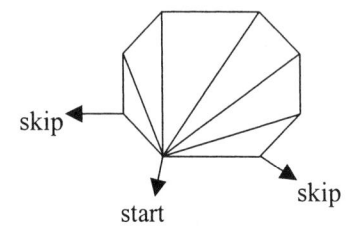

With the arrows you are taking 3 away. On the four you hold it like a diamond and then go up. You are skipping the first one and the last. I think it's 97.

KELVIN: My theory is that the answer is 97 struts because it will follow the basic pattern.

HEDDA: I like the theory to just take 3 away from the original number. Although I don't really understand any of them [very much] but I did understand that one [kind of].

These reflections highlight several important features. First, the children gave credit to others for helping them understand their theory, such as Lauren's chart or Robin's visual pattern. It is important for learners to acknowledge the explanation that most influenced their thinking; it serves as a trail to document the evolution of their thinking as well as a credit to the members of the learning community. Second, it is important that some of the children were willing to admit being skeptical, such as Derek's comment that "it would be better to see it right in front of you," or even confused by some of the other theories as Richie and Hedda were. It is not wrong or disgraceful to hold these feelings about mathematical ideas; rather, noting what makes sense provides a helpful record for tracking the thinking of learners over time; it also allows learners to hear others explain these confusing theories in perhaps new ways.

As we teachers reflected on the experience, we realized it would have been useful to have the children represent these functions on a graph, as shown in Figures 5–3a and b. Multiple forms of representation enhance one's understanding of a concept. Both graphs show a linear functional relationship and would have helped children predict the patterns that were emerging.

In the next part of this geometry experience, the children applied this new insight about triangles in an authentic context. They first looked for the use of triangles in the real world and then constructed their own designs (using straws) that would be strong and sturdy.

The Strength of Triangles: Mathematicians Connect Concepts to the Real World

The children recognized the triangle to be a "strong" shape; it was the only figure that needed no struts to make it rigid, and it also served to make other polygons rigid. Robin gave the children a homework assignment in which the children had to find examples of how triangles were used for support. They found various classroom examples, such as the easel and the triangular supports underneath tables and chairs. They also noted examples outside of class, such as bridges, radio towers, and side-door supports for automobiles. Chris found a variety of objects at his house, including the cast (and sling) for his broken arm (Figure 5–4a), while Michael shared his observation of his basketball pole and backboard

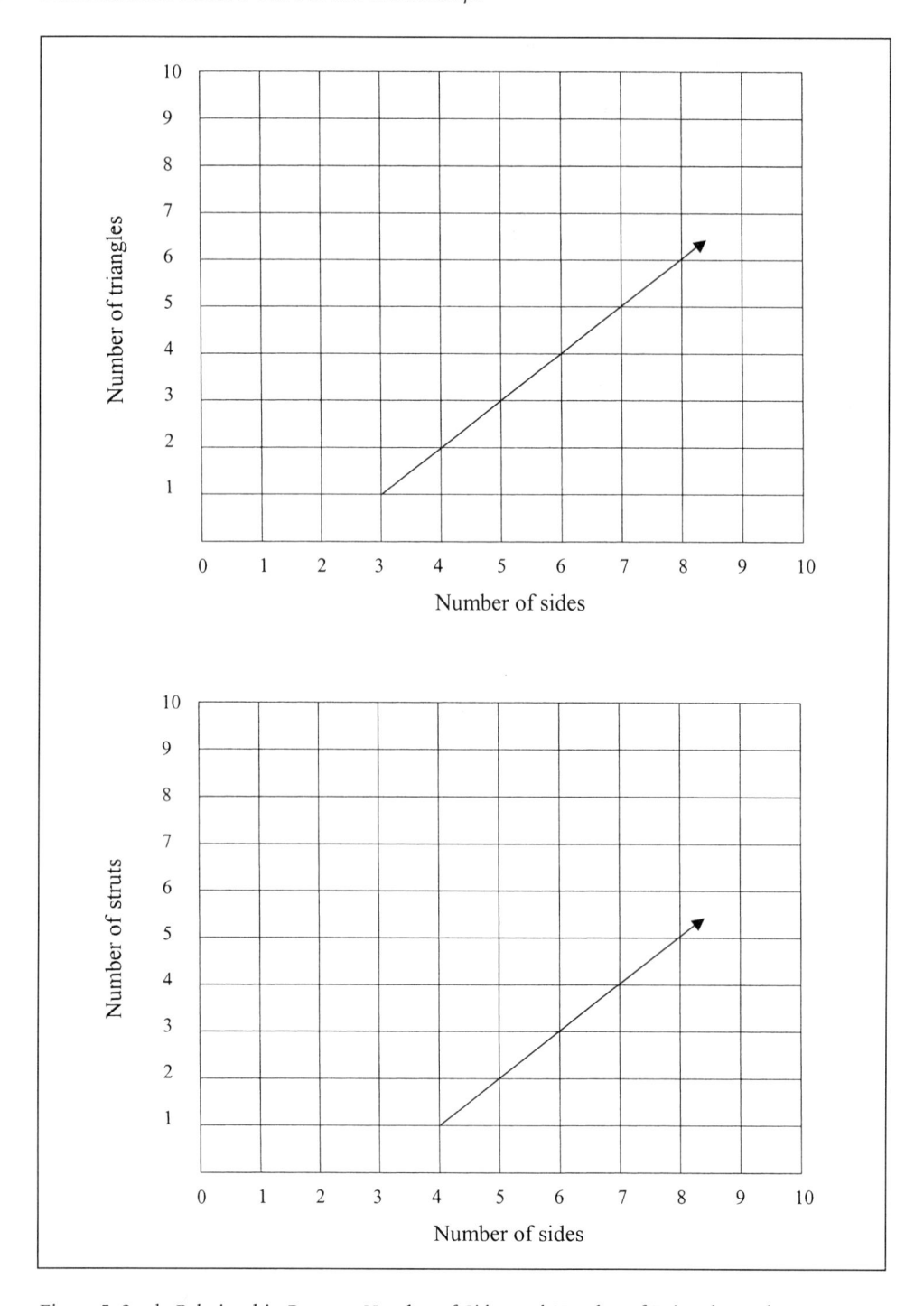

Figure 5–3a, b Relationship Between Number of Sides and Number of Triangles and Struts

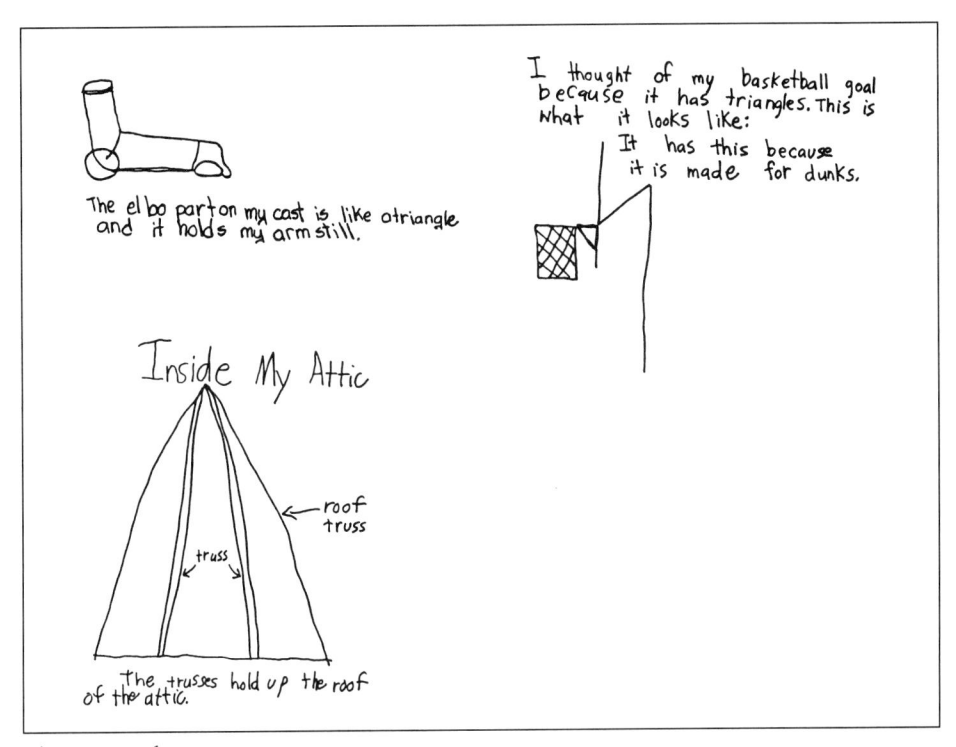

Figure 5–4a, b, c

(Figure 5–4b). Richie poked around his attic and found some other examples of triangular supports (5–4c). Brandi also noted the necessity of triangles in house construction by sharing some photographs of her own house as it was being built. Later on she wrote about what she had learned: "If it wasn't for triangles we would have a lot of problems. Like on the roof, if they didn't have a triangle roof then the water would build up and damage the roof."

Building Structures of Their Own: Mathematicians Apply Their New Knowledge

We next invited the children to put these new insights about construction to good use by building their own structures. We gave them fifteen straws, tape, and five pipe cleaners. They could slip a pipe cleaner inside two straws to help keep them together. We challenged them to build either the tallest or the strongest structure they could.

During this construction phase the children made two important connections: (1) They noticed that the changes they made in their structures were similar to the revision/composing process in writing. (2) They observed the role that triangles play in making *three*-dimensional objects strong. As the children began to work, they kept making changes in their design, trying to give more support to their structure. Several of the students compared these design changes to the kind of revisions that writers make. Jennifer wrote: "Today I worked with Leslie on architecture. First we made one and called it first draft. And then we started again and it worked out great. It was like writing a first draft, revising, and final copy."

Robin had introduced the children to various aspects of the writing process earlier in the year, which the children used during their writing workshop time. It is interesting that Jennifer related this composing process of drafts and revision to a new context—her current engineering endeavor. In this way Jennifer and her classmates were coming to see that scientific ideas, just like a writer's ideas, can be reshaped and revisited over time. We also realized that the language we use in the classroom (such as "draft" and "revision") becomes part of the collective discourse and helps to frame how learners view the world. When Jennifer tied the notion of "first draft" to the context of building, she also brought a history of previous learning experiences that demonstrated what this term meant to her. These ideas might have included, "Drafts help writers get started," "Drafts are never really final," or "Classmates can help writers revise their drafts." These ideas from writing help to support a spirit of risk taking and revision that we want to foster in this new context as well. Robin was seeing these kinds of connections between the learning of language and the learning of math, so she was pleased that some of the children were noting this parallel development as well. As we reflected further on this connection, we wondered if we ought to share the authoring cycle (Short, Harste, and Burke 1996) with the children in a more systematic way. Perhaps we should discuss some of the common strategies we use as learners across different subject areas and sign systems (e.g., language, math, art, drama). These strategies might include observing, hypothesizing, classifying, comparing, and collaborating. Jennifer's connection helped us become more reflective about our own teaching.

When Jennifer made this comparison we stopped the class, announced her connection, and invited others to note the changes they were making in their own designs. We explained that keeping track of these architectural changes was a way to follow the thinking of the designer. We feel that publicly recognizing revision as part of the composing process (whether it be building, writing, speaking, or any other form of expression) builds community. It legitimizes revision as an appropriate topic for journal writing and class discussions. All classrooms develop norms for "what we can talk about and what we can't." One of the norms that inquiry classrooms emphasize is the norm of revision, change, and tentativeness of ideas. Probably as a result of this public sharing, other students made connections to the writing process. For instance, Melanie used some of this same language of authoring to describe the process that she and her partner used to revise their structure (Figure 5–5). Brandi was careful to record changes in her design as well: "The first four arrows are for holding the third level. It was leaning but when we put 1–4 in, it made it sturdier" (Figure 5–6).

Building Structures of Their Own 99

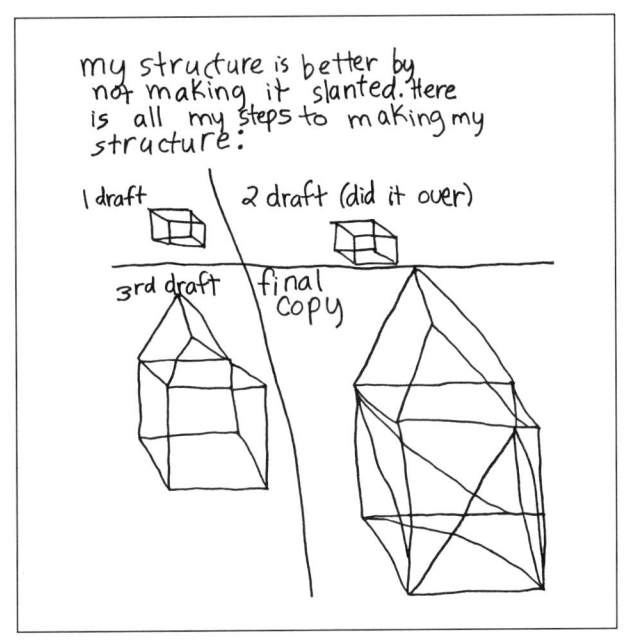

> my structure is better by not making it slanted. Here is all my steps to making my structure:
>
> 1 draft   2 draft (did it over)
>
> 3rd draft   final copy

Figure 5–5

> Changes
>
> side →
> 1st level
> 2nd level
> 3rd level
> 4 level
>
> The first 4 arrows are for holding the 3rd level. It was leaning but when we put 1-4 in it made it sturdyer.

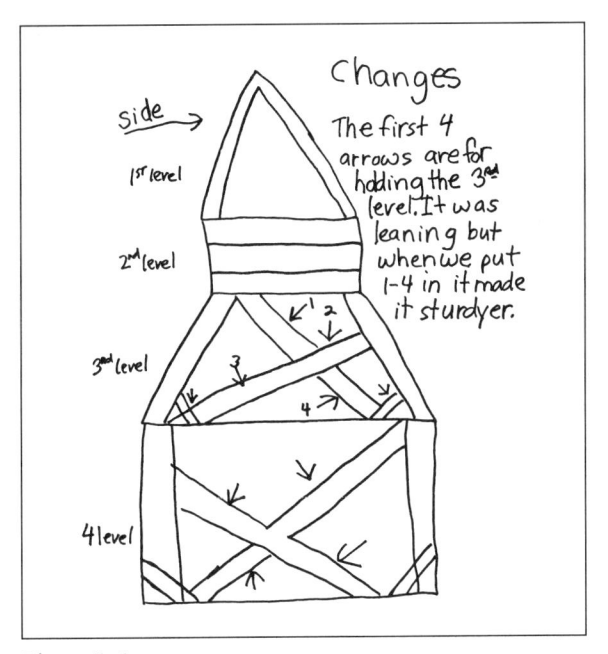

Figure 5–6

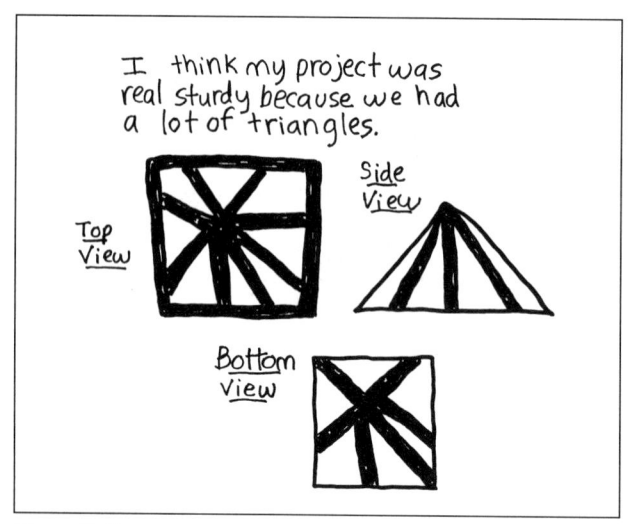

Figure 5–7

Many of the children commented about the importance of triangles to make their structure stronger. Michael wrote: "The problem we encountered was when we were making X's. We had to put them on the inside and that was hard. We made X's because you can get triangles out of an X." Aaron used many supports to make an extremely rigid construction (Figure 5–7), while Jake used interior triangular supports as well as flexible tripods on the four corners of his structure: "We changed to make [it] sturdy with triangles. We also put supports to hold [it] steady and if they need to they can go apart (Figure 5–8)." Chris B. worked with Neal to make a cube but found the structure rather weak and proposed a change. He wrote: "The first change that I could make is that we would probably use more triangles than squares. We made that mistake one time and believe me it won't happen again."

Children Reflect on Working Together

The children also wrote about the social nature of the investigation. We tried to have children regularly reflect on the process of how they learned so that the benefits of a collaborative community became more apparent to them. Robin would often ask the class, "What makes a good team of people work together well?" Supporting each other as learners in a community was her most important goal, and she worked hard to cultivate that spirit of togetherness throughout the year. However, she wanted the *children* to identify the elements that they felt were crucial in a good working relationship. Many of the comments that the other children wrote captured some of these features, such as listening, sharing ideas, crediting others for their good ideas, cooperating, persisting, and working

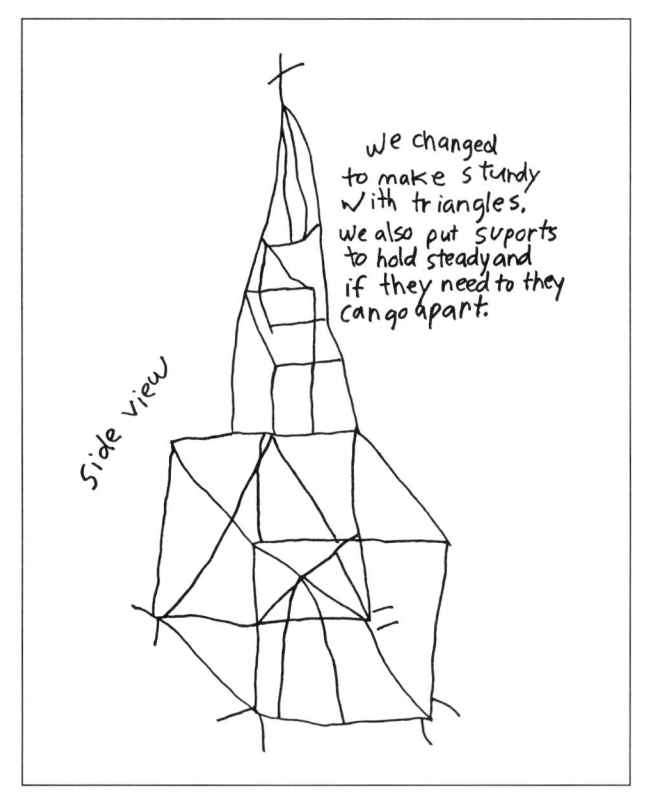

Figure 5–8

hard. We had asked them to respond to the question, "What did you learn as you worked with other people?" Here are some of their written reflections:

LESLIE: What I learned as I worked with other people was how we can work together. We got a lot done and Jennifer helped me make the architecture sturdier. Also, as I looked around the room at other buildings of straw it gave me ideas of how to build mine larger and how to make them sturdier.

LAUREN: I told Ms. Cox that it was hard. Her reply was, "That's why it's fun." And she was right. I could hardly stop.

CRYSTAL: I learned that working with someone you hardly ever work with can be as much fun as working with your best friend.

BOBBY: I learned that working with a partner you can almost do anything.

BRANDI: I really liked working with someone new. Erin knew a lot about how to keep it steady and how to get it tall. I can learn a lot from other people. Erin is a good worker and good at math.

TALITHA: I learned that if you listen and cooperate then you might get a good project. I worked with Brandon. I think he might not like this project. He didn't seem very interested when we had to start all over . . . but he worked very hard.

COLE: I learned many thing[s] today about architecture and people. About architecture sometime[s] you have to make changes in plans. People, now I know why [my partner] does not have many people that want to work with him because he will not want to work and stay on track and I made the whole thing.

As Cole's reflection indicates, sometimes there were difficulties in working together. Obviously, such comments were not read aloud to the class. Instead, Robin always kept the focus of the discussion on effective ways that teams work together. We wanted the children to realize that learning to collaborate was just as important as learning how to build a tall tower. Reflecting on the process of this working relationship helps to build a stronger community.

Investigating the Strength of Structures

Although the initial challenge was to build a structure that was either tall or sturdy, most children wanted to test its strength, particularly because they had spent so much time using triangles as supports. We therefore challenged the children to devise their own strategy for testing the strength of their design. Again, this open-ended invitation encouraged the children to test a range of methods. Most of the children used a variety of weights, such as washers and fishing weights that they brought from home, as well as some standard weights that we made available (see Figure 5–9).

Bobby described the pyramid that he and Michael built: "Michael and I did an experiment on our structure by 4,000 gm weights, and we used two of those weights and our sculpture [structure!] could hold both of those weights" (Figure 5–10). He even labeled what he considered to be the "sturdiest point" of his structure, the vertex where both the larger weights were hung. Bobby was amazed at the strength of their compact little pyramid, which was braced with many triangular supports. He traced around the perimeter of the weights he was using (a solid metal cube, and later a circular washer) and wrote "actual size wide" to convey the exact size of these weights that seemed almost as big as the structure itself!

Chris B. and Neal worked together to build a cube out of straws and then used the concepts of weight and time to determine the strength of their structure. They placed different combinations of books on top of their cube and used Chris' stopwatch to determine how long their structure supported this weight. Then they weighed the books and Chris wrote a conclusion: "This furthers my theory that the more you try the weaker it gets. I say this because it held three pounds for 12.72 seconds and only held four pounds for 8.74 seconds, so I was correct." Thus, Chris felt that the structure had been weakened by the first test and could not

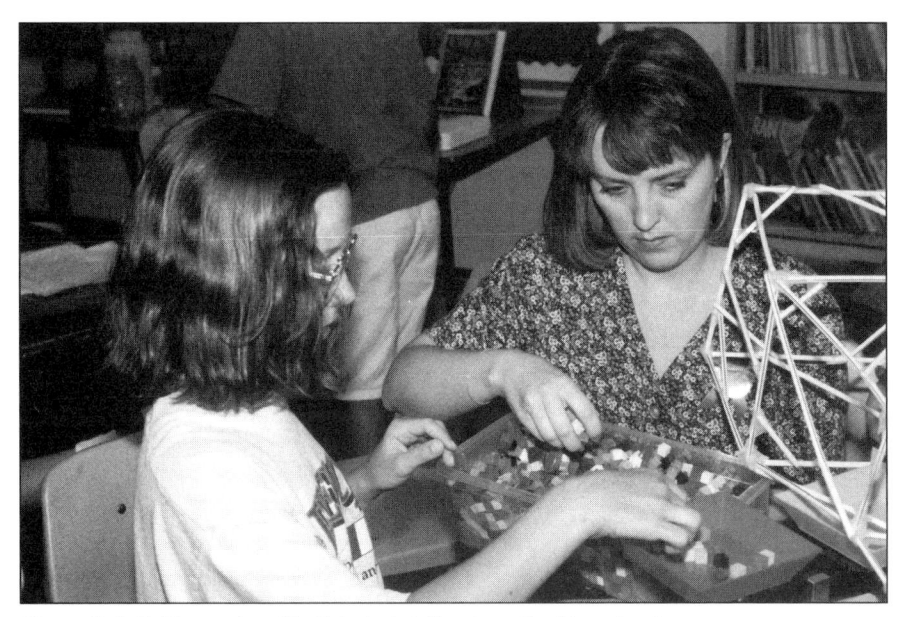

Figure 5–9 Robin works with Erin to test the strength of her structure

support the weight of the second test for as long a time. We teachers pointed out that the weight of the second test (four pounds) was greater than the weight of the first test (three pounds), and perhaps that difference in weight explained the difference in time. Chris and Neal wondered about using a different side of the cube for further testing. Unfortunately, their cube collapsed and no other tests were conducted. However, they had done an admirable job in using both these mathematical concepts of weight and time to test the strength of their design.

Since we had discussed the strength of houses in hurricanes and tornadoes (the children referred to Hurricane Hugo which had hit South Carolina several years earlier), Lauren decided to conduct an experiment to simulate those conditions (Figure 5–11). She brought in a fan from home and organized the following test. She placed her structure one foot away from the fan and one foot from the wall, turned the fan on high speed, and timed it to 50 seconds. She recorded the distance it moved. She then timed it twice more using 100-second intervals. She noted that for the first 50 seconds it moved 3 millimeters, 4 millimeters for the next 100 seconds, and 3 millimeters more for the next 100 seconds. She realized that as she continued to use the fan for each test, her structure was further away from the fan each time. After this initial test of 250 seconds the structure did not move any further. Her use of wind reminded us of a wind tunnel that engineers use to test the strength of materials and the effectiveness of certain building designs. Lauren's design provided another meaningful context for using time and distance to test the strength of a given structure.

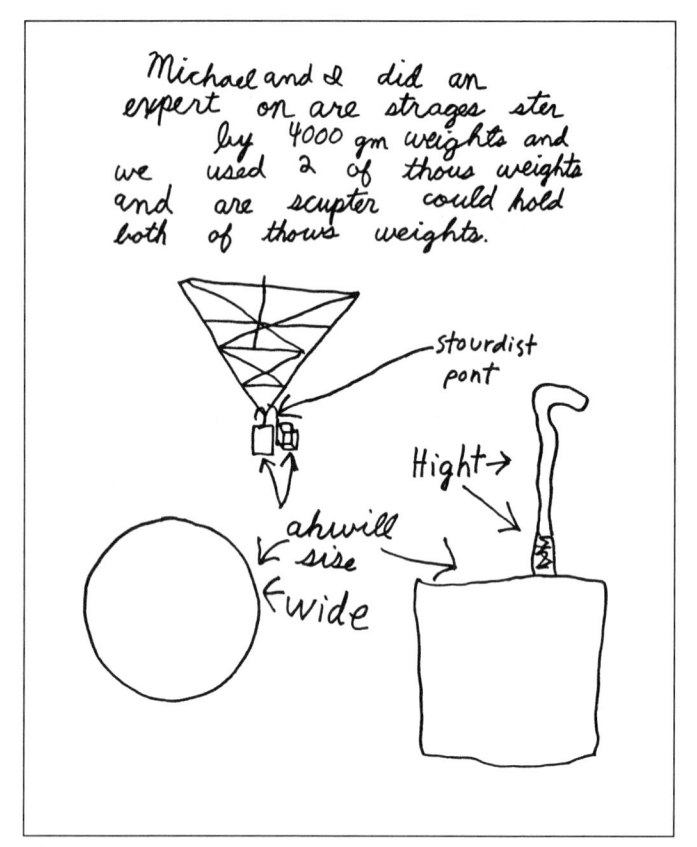

> Michael and I did an expert on are stragas ster by 4000 gm weights and we used 2 of thous weights and are scupter could hold both of thous weights.
>
> — stourdist pont
> Hight →
> ahwill
> ← sise
> ← wide

Figure 5–10

Examining the Buildings of Others

After the children had investigated the strength of triangles by designing and testing their own structures, we shared several architecture books with them. We felt their current experience would give them an appreciative yet critical eye on the buildings of others. We found this to be true, as the children reflected on these readings in their journals:

CHRIS B. (on *Man-of-War*, Biesty 1993): The way that this boat is built is truly fascinating. I mean there is so many different levels and each has a very special purpose. As time progressed each architectural design kept getting better and better to meet the needs of that time. Every compartment of a boat was very small yet they seemed to be able to fit all the supplies needed in.

CHRIS F. (on *Unbuilding*, Macaulay 1980): I noticed that they used a lot of triangles and squares, but on mine I mainly used triangles. I saw in one picture it looked

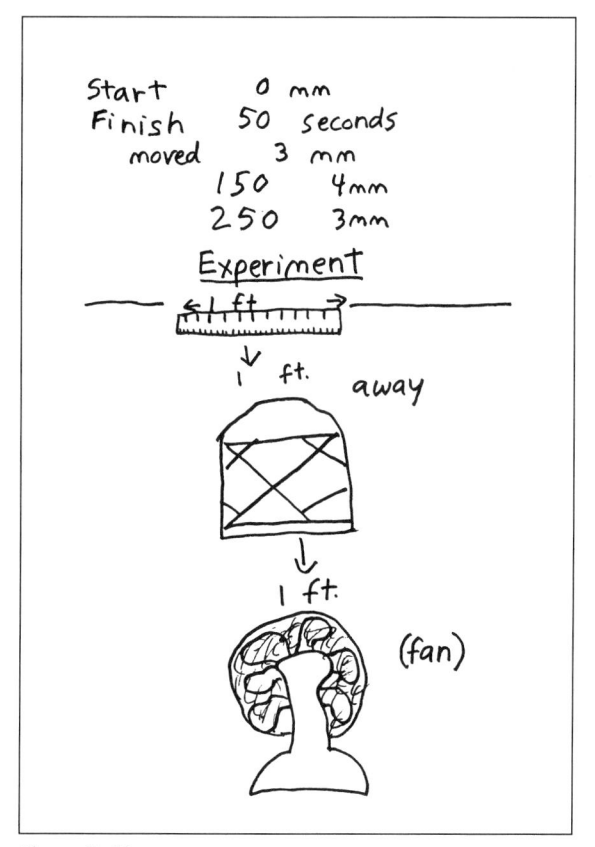

```
Start       0 mm
Finish     50 seconds
 moved      3 mm
          150  4mm
          250  3mm
         Experiment
```

Figure 5–11

like one hundred triangles. I built mine with all triangles . . . I noticed that some people used triangles in bridges.

LESLIE (on *Spiderwebs to Skyscrapers,* Darling 1991): Looking at spiderwebs, it makes me wonder how many triangles are in a spider web?

LESLIE (on *What It Feels Like to Be a Building,* Wilson 1988): This is interesting because it says beams cannot bend too much because they would split down the middle. And then it says that's why roofs supported by beams are flat. So next time I'll remember to make the roof of my straw building flatter. I observed that arches have different shapes and designs. I wonder if that has anything to do with how sturdy it is.

MICHAEL (on *Houses and Homes,* Morris 1992): One can learn good design by purposely doing poor design.

TALITHA (on *Cathedral,* Macaulay 1973): I learned that people build buildings in different ways . . . They tied pieces together, put cement on pieces, and they even built with triangles. I was surprised that they even had triangular bricks! I learned that circles and ovals are also important in a building.

The children read these books with enlightened eyes because they viewed themselves as builders. They connected several pieces of architecture to their own designs, especially the use of triangles. However, they found triangles in new places, such as bridges, and noted other shapes that give support, such as circles and columns. Their observations even led to further wonders, such as the strength of spider webs and the design of other animal structures. Later in the year the children found other examples of engineering principles during their trip to Charleston. The noticed the many triangular supports on the bridges. They learned about the iron supports that were placed in buildings and homes to minimize damage during earthquakes. They learned the benefit of strategically positioning porches to catch the cool sea breezes during the summer heat. Last, they learned about the design of some new homes that have curved exterior walls to lessen the force of hurricane winds.

Reflecting on the Experience with Triangles

As we reflected on this series of geometry experiences we were reminded of the important role of language in explaining and exploring mathematical patterns. It was through conversations that we were building a supportive, collaborative mathematics community. Learners used these class discussions to pose wonders, share strategies, and admit confusions. It was also a time to raise questions, build arguments, and refute theories. We realized that the teacher's role was crucial for encouraging this diversity of voices. We needed to insist that children explain their thinking, respond to the differing viewpoints of others, and make sense of their experience in their own way. We realized that we, too, must remain divergent thinkers by continuing to entertain children's alternative theories or interpretations. We were all learning, and we were doing it together—and that's probably the biggest lesson of all.

Going Beyond the Experience

1. Encourage children to reflect regularly on how their group/partner worked together successfully. Post a chart in the room that lists these effective strategies and continue to add new insights as the year progresses.

2. Invite children to investigate *why* things are shaped the way they are. For instance, why are manhole covers round, or coat hangers triangular (and specifically isosceles), or card tables square? They might inquire why things in nature are shaped the way they are. For instance, why are the root systems of plants and trees circular, or why are the cells of a honeycomb hexagonal? They might even compare and contrast

natural and manufactured shapes. Catherine Ross has written an excellent series of books related to this idea: *Triangles* (1994), *Squares* (1996), and *Circles* (1992).

3. Highlight revision as a natural part of the composing process, not only in writing, but also in all areas of the curriculum. Look for instances where children revise their thinking and encourage them to record that process in their journal as well as share it with the class. Post a chart in the room that documents these examples of revision, what prompted the revision, and what each child learned from the experience.

4. Encourage children to reflect on the benefits of a classroom conversation: How did the conversation help you grow as a learner? What did a classmate say that you found interesting? How did the idea of a classmate give you a new idea? Regular reflections on conversations help children develop an appreciation for the power of talk in a collaborative community.

5. Invite an engineer to class to discuss principles of design. Why are buildings constructed the way they are? What are the forces that engineers must keep in mind as they design buildings? (Currently, there is much debate about the structural integrity of skyscrapers and other tall buildings.)

Notes: Clarification from a University Colleague

We spoke to Rheta Rubenstein, a mathematics educator at the University of Michigan–Dearborn, about ratios and functions. She explained that a function is a rule in which every input has only one output. The "Guess My Rule" game is a good example of how a function operates. For instance, here are some numbers that get changed by going in one box and coming out another box:

In	Out
5	8
12	15
38	41

The function is following a "plus 3" rule. Children can create various rules to challenge their peers, including rules that require two operations, such as:

In	Out
5	20
9	40
2	5

In this case the rule is to multiply the input by 5, then subtract 5 from that product. A ratio is an example of proportional reasoning and is often expressed as $y = (k)x$, where k is the constant. A ratio is an ordered pair of numbers that express a comparison between those numbers. A good example of this kind of relationship is $C = \pi \times d$, where π is the constant. This constant can also be expressed as a ratio of c/d. In the strut problem, for instance, David G. was naming 5 sides and 2 struts as a 5:2 ratio. He then used this ratio to establish a proportion, which is a statement of equality between two ratios: If 5:2, then 10:4. However, he needed to consider all the numbers in the chart before deciding that this was a proportional situation. The numbers on the chart represented a *non*proportional, or additive context; that is, every time one more side wa*s added* to the polygon, one more strut was added to make the shape rigid. Multiplying a 4-sided shape by 2 (a constant) to get an 8-sided shape does not express the additive increase of struts that was occurring. Several children refuted this theory of a ratio relationship by arguing that what *was* constant was that the number of struts was always 3 fewer than the number of sides.

6 Developing a Math Workshop

We wanted to continue to foster this spirit of mathematical exploration by developing a math workshop where children could investigate their own mathematical questions. Robin had asked herself, "If I can develop a workshop time for reading and writing, why can't I do the same for math?" We envisioned that the children would have a choice in what they pursued and extended periods of time to explore those choices. NCTM has argued that learners need regular, large blocks of time to delve into various mathematical projects (NCTM 2000). We felt that a math workshop time could foster a healthy persistence in tackling new problems without the pressure of having to complete them in a single class period. We were also convinced that personal choice in mathematics is just as important as it is in reading and writing. Children's ownership of their own investigation instills a certain responsibility for persevering and carrying the task to its completion. We also felt a math workshop time would demonstrate to children that mathematics is a way of thinking and viewing the world, and is naturally embedded in many different contexts. We were convinced that a wide range of projects would naturally integrate and connect various concepts and strategies. This connectedness is an important process standard advocated by NCTM.

Before we look closely at some of the children's experiences during math workshop, Robin will share her personal reflections about this time. Following is her response to some basic questions about the workshop.

You developed a math workshop for your students. Why did you do this and how did you organize it? How did this workshop time fit in with the district math curriculum?

I developed a math workshop because I wanted to see if the children could apply the skills they were learning. I started this workshop during the second part of the year. We used our regular math time for this, and we would devote two to three sessions a week to workshop. However, the time would vary. There might be a three-week period when we didn't have workshop at all because of concerts, field trips, and other things that can crowd the schedule. But I did enjoy the times we held workshop because it gave kids tremendous choice in what they wanted to pursue. They all knew that their project had to have a mathematical focus, but they could find ideas almost anywhere.

As a way to ease into the new workshop, we did some whole-class explorations first. For instance, we would do some basic measurements of pumpkins and then brainstorm how we might use these measurements to explore additional relationships (discussed in Chapter 2). On another occasion we investigated money by looking at which Federal Reserve Bank issued the dollar bills we collected. (The name of the city is written on the insignia on the front of the bill.) Children developed different theories for why certain cities appeared more frequently, such as distance from our state, size of population, number of tourist attractions, and so on. It was a wonderful interdisciplinary project because it got kids looking at maps, reading scale drawings, and using a variety of resources. There was this initial engagement of collecting the data together, and then we brainstormed individual extensions from this initial data. Projects like these built the groundwork for math workshop later on.

One of the things I most liked about math workshop is that the children had to decide what tools to use to solve their problem. I had a variety of tools for them to use: scales, measuring tapes, calculators, geometric pieces, and so on. But the children had to decide what to use to help them with their particular project. I have always felt that schools rob kids of good learning opportunities when they tell them what materials they will need ahead of time. Inquiry learning means deciding for yourself what tools you need. One of my students, Bobby, needed to measure the length of the hallway and chose a ruler for his tool. As he talked with me afterwards, he realized that the 100-foot tape would have been a more appropriate tool. Workshop time gave me opportunities like this to teach some minilessons to students. During the currency investigation I taught some children how to determine miles using a map scale. I helped others learn to use an almanac to find the populations of states. And then there was Lauren, who gathered data from her classmates on what TV channel they watched the most. She was curious to see if her results matched the ratings that were announced by a local TV network. At my urging she called the station, but the receptionist told her that her teacher really needed to call for that information. Lauren and I discussed how she could be more assertive on the phone. She needed a way to get past the receptionist and talk directly to the person responsible for calculating the ratings. She did call back, asked for the appropriate person, shared her findings, and asked some important questions about their data. Here was an example of a minilesson on phone etiquette. And all of these minilessons were directly related to my district skills in math and language, such as reading scales, identifying appropriate resources, and communicating effectively with different audiences. I make sure that I am very familiar with all these skills and then look for their emergence during this math workshop time. I find kids learn these skills best when they are using them for a purpose.

Laying the Groundwork for the Math Workshop

Another effective strategy for getting started was sharing the book *Counting on Frank* (Clement 1991). As discussed in Chapter 1, this book demonstrates what it means to think mathematically. It also fosters a mathematical musing about the world by emphasizing the word "if." The investigations that the children carried out with pumpkins were certainly the roots of our math workshop. Although everyone was asking questions about pumpkins, they posed questions that were interesting to them and devised appropriate strategies to solve them. We also used *Counting on Frank* as a catalyst for children to pose their own questions. For instance, Robert devised the question, "How many Eyewitness Books will fit in our study bookcase?" (Figure 6–1). He measured the width of each book and length of the bookcase to calculate the number of books per shelf. He then counted the number of shelves and columns and multiplied to determine the total. Brent

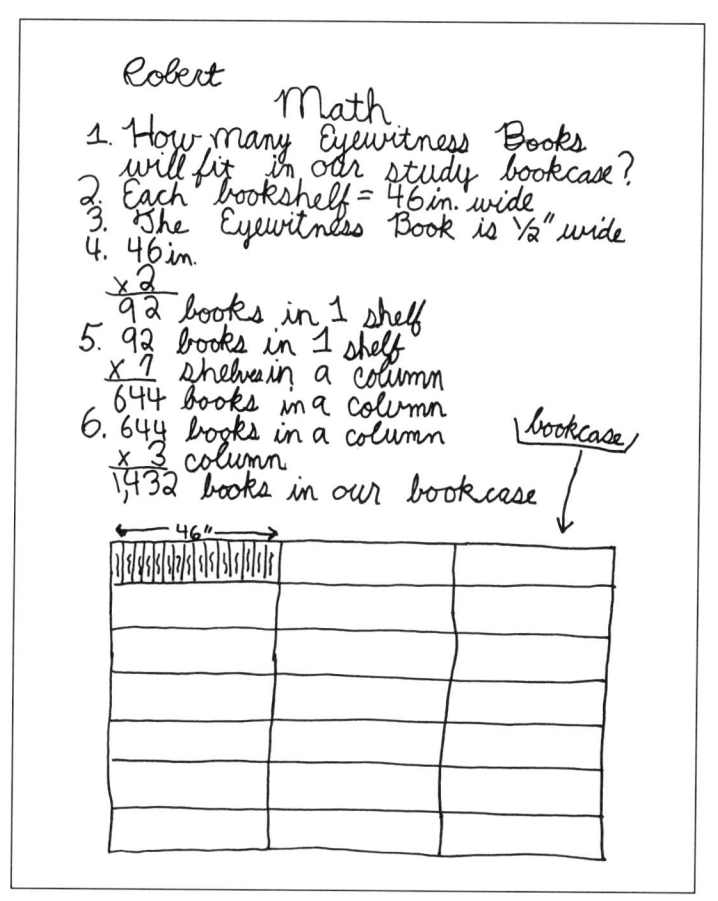

Figure 6–1

wanted to find out the number of beds that could fit into his bedroom (Figure 6–2). He measured both his bed and the room and divided to obtain his result. One of the purposes of these early investigations was for children to see that mathematical possibilities are all around them. Developing this mathematical habit of mind was an important precursor to the math workshop that was to follow later in the year.

Another strategy that we used at the beginning of the year was to share a statistic with the children and ask them to respond to it. We used several statistics from *In an Average Lifetime . . .* (Heymann 1992). We posted the statistic on the board, asked children to copy it in their journals, and then had them write about what they found interesting or what they wondered about after reading it. For instance, the first statistic that Robin posted was, "The average American lives to be 74.9 years of age. That gives each of us 899 months; 27,339 days; 656,136 hours; or 39,368,160 minutes to sleep, eat, work, play, or otherwise pass time."

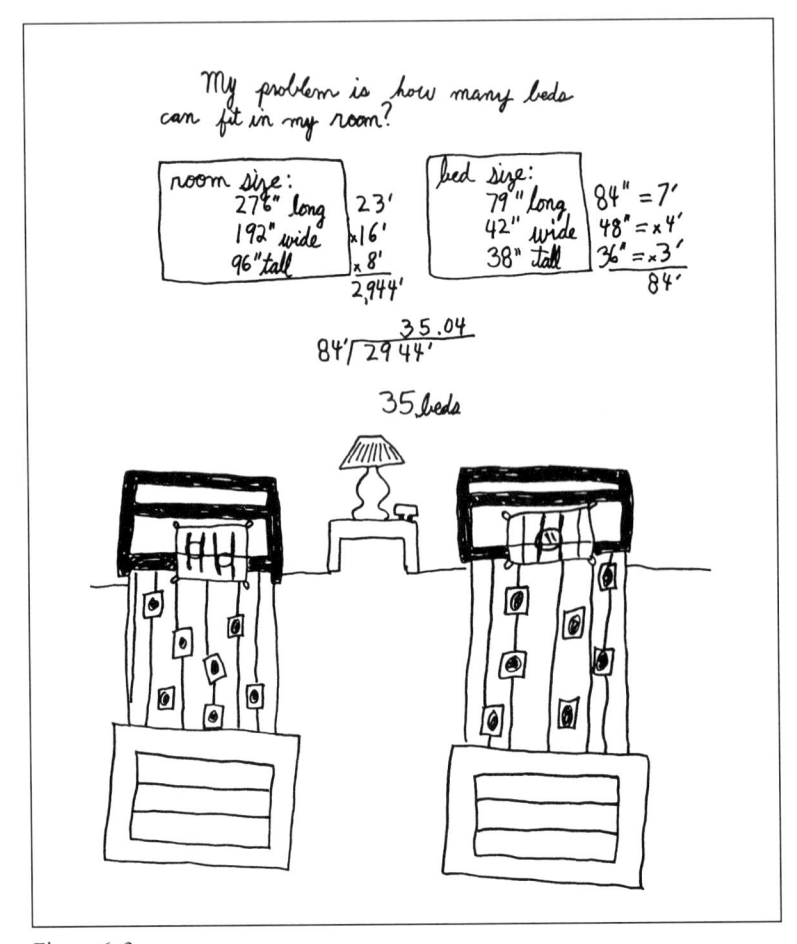

Figure 6–2

The children generated questions in their journals, such as: "What is the average lifetime of a frog?" and "How old would I be if I lived a million seconds?" The statistic also inspired some philosophical reflections, such as, "When you take a glance at it our life is short, but if you look good [closely] at it, it is not."

We then had a class discussion about this statistic. When Kelvin shared his interest in seconds, David W. shared the measure of a nanosecond (one-millionth of a second); this particular unit of time intrigued several students who later pursued the topic on their own. Most of the questions that the children posed were not investigated any further. However, that was not our intent. We were trying to encourage children to question, revise, and extend data; we wanted to foster a curiosity about data so that any statistic could be the seed for further study and investigation. When we later shared another statistic, the children posed even more questions. The statistic read: "The average American celebrates 74 birthdays, receives 333 birthday presents, receives 2,322 greeting cards, and of these, 524 are birthday cards." Here are some of the children's questions:

- How many hours does the average person sleep?
- How long does it take to go around the world in a plane nonstop?
- How many report cards does an average person get?
- How many hours do you watch TV?
- How big can trees get in two years?
- How many heartbeats does a person have in a lifetime?
- What's the average number of hours that you play video games?
- You could calculate how many hours you play or work, or how many hours you write or read, or how many hours you are in school or at home.
- How much money is spent on a person each year (average)?
- How many vacations do you go on in your life?
- How many times do you walk through your living room?
- How many kids in District Five like school?
- How long would your hair be if you did not cut it for a year?

We felt that our discussions about *Counting on Frank*, our pumpkin investigations, and our questions about statistics provided some important groundwork for the math workshop. We then discussed our plan for a math workshop with the class and invited them to think of mathematical questions that they might wish to pursue. They could select a question that they generated from our discussion about statistics; they might look through other books on statistics, such as *The Guinness Book of World Records* (Cunningham 1992), and find interesting facts that they could investigate in some way; they could gather their own data from classmates about a topic they found interesting; they might choose a literature book that had a mathematical dimension to it (Whitin and Wilde, 1992, 1995) and investigate an appealing facet of that story; or they might pose a question that involved the use of one of the manipulative materials in the room, such as the pattern blocks or base blocks (which included several other bases in addition to base 10). Since we presented them with a number of options, their initial choices reflected this diversity:

Chris, Kelvin:	What is the largest potato chip in the world? How many regular size chips would fit inside the big one?
Cole, Talitha, Jennifer:	Is it possible to build a base 11 block?
Erin, Chris B.:	How long does it really take to count to one million?
Colby, Greg:	How many nanoseconds are there in an hour?
Michael, Richard:	How many heartbeats are there in a lifetime? How many minutes do we watch TV in a lifetime?
Brandi, Jake:	How many movies do people see? How much time do people spend reading?
Melanie, Leslie, Crystal:	How many units (cm. cubes) does it take to fill up the liter container?
Brandon:	What is the circumference of people's necks? Does the size of your shoe matter how high you jump?

As the year progressed, still other questions emerged:

Brandi, Chase:	What is the average height of people in our class?
Richie:	How many people die in one year?
Derek:	How long would it take a jet to travel around the world?
Bobby:	How big is the flag at Fort McHenry compared to other things?
Cole:	How many pattern blocks does it take to make bigger blocks?
Melanie:	What are the best items for us to sell at the school store?
Chase, Neal:	What is the average points a basketball player scores?
Brandon, Timothy, Aaron:	What is the number of touchdowns that each NFL team scores?
Crystal, Hedda, Leslie:	What different bases can fit into the liter container?

Math workshop ran about two afternoons a week for approximately sixty to seventy-five minutes. In the rest of this chapter we will share some of the children's projects and the ways they solved their problems and shared their information. We believe that a closer look at some of these projects will affirm the potential for developing a math workshop. We will close the chapter by highlighting the benefits of this math workshop time as well as suggesting ways to refine it.

We devised a series of questions that we wanted the children to use in reflecting on their math project. Children responded to these two questions after every math workshop:

1. What did you learn today?
2. What do you still wonder about?

Children chose some of the following questions to answer when they finished a mathematical exploration:

1. Who would find this information useful? Why?
2. What surprised you about what you found out? Why?
3. What is another way you could have explored your idea?
4. How did you solve any problems you encountered?
5. What did you learn as you worked with other people?
6. What changes would you make if you did this project again? Why would you make these changes?
7. What are some "what if" questions you could now ask about your project?
8. What did you learn about yourself as a learner after having done this project?
9. What did you learn about mathematics after having done this project?
10. What kind of questions does your project *not* answer?

The questions focused on the process of their investigation, including their own individual attitudes, as well as their work with peers. We included the last question, "What kind of questions does your project *not* answer?" because we wanted to emphasize again that investigations never end. One question may get answered, only to raise further questions.

Robin also developed a workshop evaluation form (see page 116). She felt it was important for children to reflect on the quality of their work and how well they used their time.

Pursuing Heartbeats, Deaths, and Nanoseconds

Michael was intrigued with the statistics we had shared about the average American and wanted to find out the number of heartbeats in a lifetime. To get started, he took the pulse of most of the people in the class and found the average of 70.2 beats per minute. He used a calculator to continue his problem solving:

> **Math Workshop Evaluation**
>
> Directions: On a scale of 1–10, rate yourself on the following criteria. Remember, in order to receive a 10, you must ALWAYS meet the criteria.
>
> 1. I always work hard during math workshop and do not waste a lot of time talking and playing around. _____
> 2. When others give me suggestions, I listen to them and give their suggestions some thought. _____
> 3. If someone asks me a question or tries to get my response to a survey, I am cooperative and try to answer. _____
> 4. I write in my journal at the end of every math workshop and whenever I finish an exploration. _____
> 5. I work at home on my explorations. I am willing to be independent and do some work on my own. _____
> 6. I always clean up my area and put my materials away. _____
> 7. I help others clean up as well. _____
> 8. I do an overall quality job in math workshop and care very much about my time to explore. _____
> 9. My visuals and other products are always done to the best of my ability. _____

$$70.2 \text{ beats per minute} \times 60 = 4{,}212 \text{ beats per hour}$$
$$4{,}212 \times 24 = 101{,}088 \text{ beats per day}$$
$$101{,}088 \times 365 = 36{,}897{,}120 \text{ beats per year}$$

He then tried to multiply 36,897,120 by 74 years but found that the calculator could not hold that many digits. He cleverly used the distributive property to solve his problem; he multiplied 36,897,120 by 7 and then multiplied by 10 (adding a zero to his answer) to determine the number of beats in 70 years. He then multiplied the yearly figure by 4 and added the two figures together:

$$36{,}897{,}120 \times 7 = 2{,}582{,}798{,}400 = \text{beats in 70 years}$$
$$36{,}897{,}120 \times 4 = 147{,}588{,}480 = \text{beats in 4 years}$$
$$2{,}730{,}386{,}880 = \text{beats in 74 years}$$

When Michael shared his results with the class Crystal asked him, "What if your heart stopped beating, or what if it started going faster?" Michael responded,

"If your heart never stops, and never goes faster, this is what it would be. It's the average." When Robin asked him to explain what he meant by average, he said, "It's not the exact number of heartbeats; it's the average." Thus, Michael (with the help of Crystal) was contributing to the class' understanding of the benefits of an average, that is, it gives an approximation for understanding a situation or event. Michael became so fascinated with his answer that he went on to calculate the number of heartbeats in 100 years, 500 years, 1,000 years, and even 20,000 years! While this kind of calculating may seem tedious and boring at first, it certainly was not a chore for Michael. He worked with much intensity and diligence during several workshop times to complete his calculations, and was quite pleased with his efforts. What was so appealing about this project for Michael? David M. Schwartz, author of *How Much Is a Million?* (1985) and *If You Made a Million* (1989), commented that children seem to enjoy large numbers much as they do other large things, such as the enormity of dinosaurs or the vastness of outer space (Whitin and Wilde 1995). We found this to be true. Some children seemed mesmerized by the magnitude of large numbers and developed projects that allowed them to pursue this interest.

Colby and Greg were also enamored of large numbers and wanted to investigate the number of nanoseconds in an hour. Their calculations extended their understanding of place value and their ability to read large numbers. When asked why he chose this question, Colby remarked, "I like to add up large numbers." The boys began by figuring the number of nanoseconds in one minute (i.e., 60,000,000) and then used the three minutes total for the first entry on their chart (Figure 6–3). They counted by two-minute intervals and added 120,000,000 nanoseconds each time. When they reached the fifty-ninth minute they added only 60,000,000 more nanoseconds to determine the final total of 3,600,000,000 nanoseconds! They even went on to calculate the number of nanoseconds in a day and in a week.

Richie confronted some large numbers when he wanted to know the number of people who died in one year. He looked in several almanacs and finally found this ratio: 10 deaths per 1,000 people worldwide. He then found the population of the world: 5,292,000,000 inhabitants. (It is now over 6 billion). As he talked to David W. during this point in his investigation, he was not quite sure how to proceed:

DAVID W.: Now that you know these facts, what are you going to do next to find out how many people die in one year?

RICHIE: We could do 1,000 times 5,292,000,000.

DAVID W.: Why would that make sense?

RICHIE: Well, no . . . yeah. It might. But then over here it says 10 people for each 1,000. So we could see how many thousands in that. So 5,292,000,000 divided by 1,000.

DAVID W.: What would that tell us?

118   *Developing a Math Workshop*

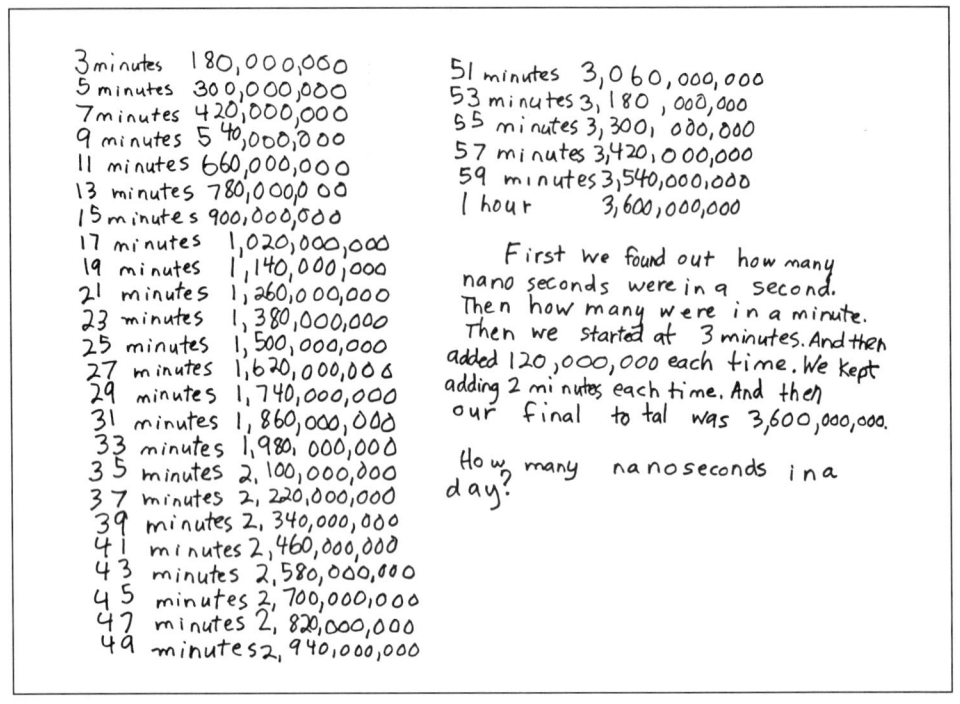

```
3 minutes    180,000,000         51 minutes  3,060,000,000
5 minutes    300,000,000         53 minutes  3,180,000,000
7 minutes    420,000,000         55 minutes  3,300,000,000
9 minutes    540,000,000         57 minutes  3,420,000,000
11 minutes   660,000,000         59 minutes  3,540,000,000
13 minutes   780,000,000         1 hour      3,600,000,000
15 minutes   900,000,000
17 minutes   1,020,000,000       First we found out how many
19 minutes   1,140,000,000    nano seconds were in a second.
21 minutes   1,260,000,000    Then how many were in a minute.
23 minutes   1,380,000,000    Then we started at 3 minutes. And then
25 minutes   1,500,000,000    added 120,000,000 each time. We kept
27 minutes   1,620,000,000    adding 2 minutes each time. And then
29 minutes   1,740,000,000    our final total was 3,600,000,000.
31 minutes   1,860,000,000
33 minutes   1,980,000,000    How many nanoseconds in a
35 minutes   2,100,000,000    day?
37 minutes   2,220,000,000
39 minutes   2,340,000,000
41 minutes   2,460,000,000
43 minutes   2,580,000,000
45 minutes   2,700,000,000
47 minutes   2,820,000,000
49 minutes   2,940,000,000
```

Figure 6–3

RICHIE: How many thousands there are. And then we could divide that by 10 because there's 10 people for each 1,000.

Richie and David W. then discussed that if there were 10 people per 1,000, then multiplying (not dividing) 10 people for each 1,000 would yield the total number of people who die in one year. He said he wanted to really understand just how large that number was but he wasn't sure how to do that. David W. suggested comparing that number to the total number of people in the United States. Based on a population of 250 million (although it's actually over 260 million now), Richie saw quite readily that approximately 50 million deaths was the same as almost one-fifth of all the people in the United States. He then wanted his classmates to better understand the population of the United States, so he compared that population to South Carolina's and found it would take 76½ South Carolina populations to equal the population of the United States.

Richie's investigation raises several important points. First, the availability of a calculator enabled Richie to pursue this question; one of the advantages of using a calculator in the classroom is that it allows learners to explore a wide range of problems that before were not accessible because of the detailed computations needed. Second, an important question to ask learners as they explain their thinking is, "Why does that make sense to you to do it that way?" That response legitimizes children as sense makers and supports them to explain their reasoning. It is a helpful question to ask in response to expected responses, as well as unexpected ones.

The other interesting feature of Richie's exploration was his insistence on making some mathematical comparisons so his figures might be better understood by his audience (and himself!). Comparing is a useful mathematical strategy because it enables learners to understand the relative size of things and thereby make better sense of numerical data. We believe that parts of Richie's interest in making comparisons stemmed from the emphasis we placed on this strategy early in the year. We read several books to the class—*How Much Is a Million?* (Schwartz 1985), *Large as Life Animals* (Cole 1985), and *The Book of Animal Records* (Drew 1989)—and then posted on large charts the mathematical comparisons that the children found most interesting. This table shows some of these comparisons:

Comparison Statement	Mathematical Concept
One anaconda weighs as much as three humans.	Weight, equivalence
A human being can only run half as fast as a cheetah.	Time, length
The legs of a royal antelope are as thin as pencils, and all four of its hoof prints could fit on a fifty-cent piece.	Area
A squirrel monkey can fit inside your school bag.	Volume
A million goldfish need as much water as it takes to hold a whale.	Capacity
A billion kids standing on each other's shoulders could be longer than the distance from the earth to the moon.	Length

When we asked the children to explain the advantages of mathematical comparisons, they listed several: "It's easier to understand"; "It makes it more interesting"; "It tells us how big things are in things that we see and use every day." Comparisons act as reference points, or benchmarks, for understanding the relative size and magnitude of things in our world; they encompass all mathematical concepts and cut across all subject fields. Several of the children used this strategy of comparing as the basis for their math projects. The following investigation by Chris B. and Kelvin provided one such example.

Exploring the Largest Potato Chip and the Largest Stamp

After we had shared several statistics about the average American, we also suggested the *Guinness Book of World Records* (Cunningham 1992) as another source of statistics that the children might want to use in an investigation. Chris B. and

Kelvin looked through this resource book and found the record for the largest potato chip in the world (14½ inches long, made by Pringles). This statistic intrigued Chris B. because he often brought potato chips to school as part of his lunch. They decided to compare this large chip to their regular-size chips and found the large chip to be about 4½ times larger. Since they only had length to go by, they had to estimate the area of the chip. They drew the contour lines of this large chip and placed the smaller chip inside this area. They enjoyed this project so much that they decided to figure out "how many of the stamps we have will go into the biggest stamp in the world." They drew a model of this largest stamp on a piece of notebook paper and then laid their stamps down on top of it (Figure 6–4). They noticed that four spaces on this paper covered one stamp, so they calculated how to combine the remaining spaces at the bottom of the paper to make additional stamps. Chris B. wrote: "Each stamp is four spaces of notebook paper down, but when you get to the bottom of the stamp there is only three spaces instead of the four needed so we borrowed and out of four uncompleted stamps we got three full stamps. On the side it is not completed so I estimated that if you add all four spaces up that they would make one full stamp." Thus, they were using the concept of area, the strategy of estimating, and the skill of adding fractional parts to solve their own problem.

How Long Does It Take a Jet to Go Around the World?

Another interesting project that involved the strategy of comparing was Derek's investigation of "How long does it take a jet to go around the world?" The impetus for this project grew out of an "expert project" that Brandi had done early in the year. Robin had invited the children to explore a topic that was interesting to them. Brandi had decided to study jets. She interviewed fighter pilots, visited the local Air National Guard base, read everything that she could on jets, and built a model of a jet. Derek was intrigued with her project and asked her numerous questions about jets and their capabilities. Thus, it was no surprise later in the year that Derek wanted to do a mathematical investigation about jets. Derek's extension of Brandi's report demonstrated to us again the value of children sharing their projects with each other.

He began his project by trying to calculate the distance around the globe. He used a cloth tape to measure around the equator of the globe and found it to be 38 inches. David W. pointed out the mileage key on the globe and Derek found that one inch represented 660 miles. He used the calculator to determine the circumference of the earth: 660 miles per inch × 38 inches = 25,080 miles. He then realized he needed to know the speed of jets, so he asked Brandi. She responded, "What kind of jet?" Derek asked, "How many are there?" "There is a hypersonic, supersonic, and a regular jet," she explained. "Well, give me the information on all three," he said. Since Brandi gave him a range of speeds for each jet (regular jet, 200–500 mph; supersonic jet, 1,000–4,000 mph; hypersonic jet, 4,000–8,000 mph), Derek decided to use "the middle speed" (a wonderful way to describe an

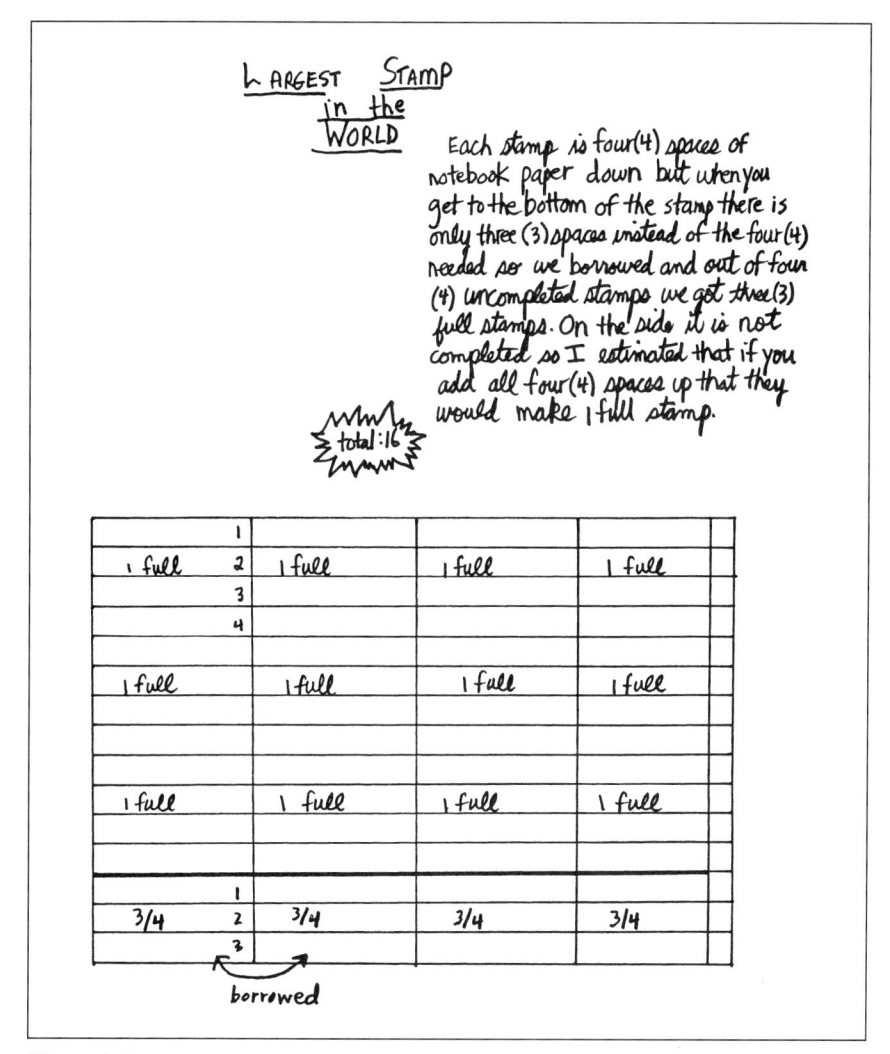

> **LARGEST STAMP in the WORLD**
>
> Each stamp is four(4) spaces of notebook paper down but when you get to the bottom of the stamp there is only three(3) spaces instead of the four(4) needed so we borrowed and out of four(4) uncompleted stamps we got three(3) full stamps. On the side it is not completed so I estimated that if you add all four(4) spaces up that they would make 1 full stamp.
>
> total: 16
>
> | 1 full | 1 full | 1 full | 1 full |
> |---|---|---|---|
> | 1 full | 1 full | 1 full | 1 full |
> | 1 full | 1 full | 1 full | 1 full |
> | 3/4 | 3/4 | 3/4 | 3/4 |
>
> borrowed

Figure 6–4

average) as a basis for his calculations. With the help of a calculator Derek figured out the amount of time each jet would need to circle the earth once. He then wanted to express these times using a more familiar context. Like Chris B. and Kelvin had earlier, he used the strategy of comparing to make his data more understandable (Figure 6–5): "If you got a long weekend, like three days, it would take a regular jet one hour less than three days to go around the world. If you went around the world in a hypersonic jet it would take 2/3 of a school day. Your parents probably tell you to get eight hours of sleep or more. If you got eight hours

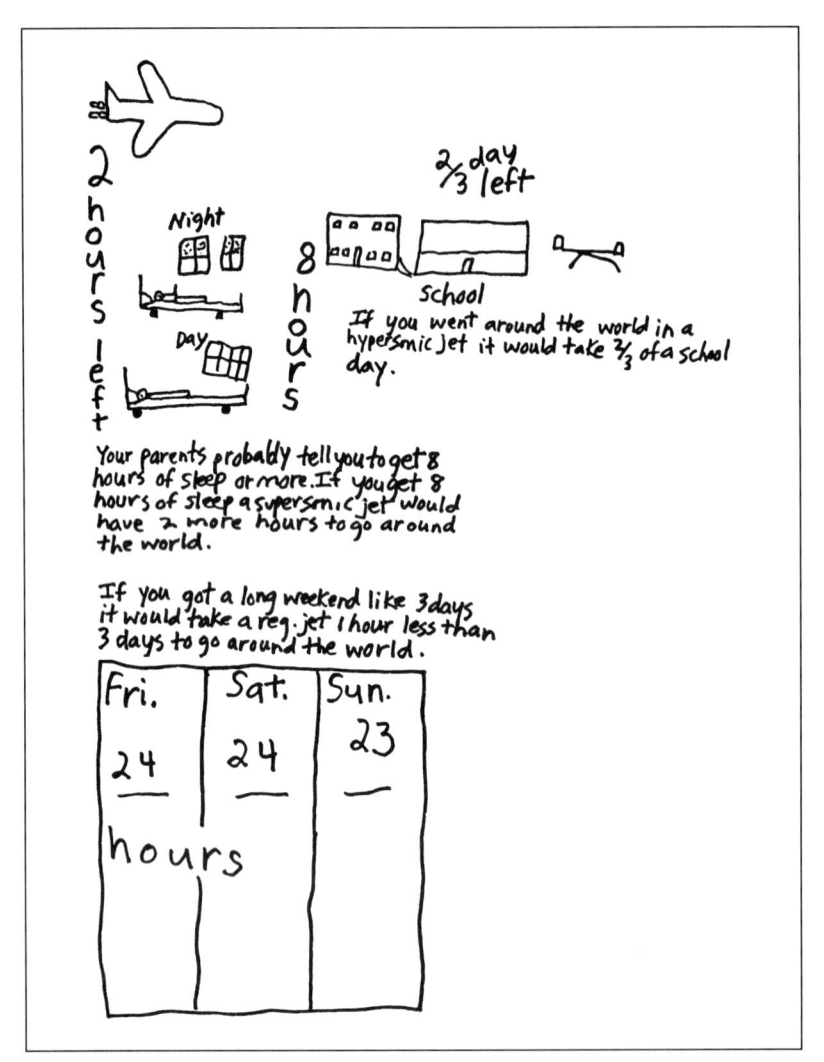

Figure 6–5

then a supersonic jet would have two more hours to go around the world." Thus, Derek used appropriate mathematical comparisons that he felt connected to his audience's experiences. His writing reflects NCTM's Communication Standard in which "students communicate their mathematical thinking coherently and clearly to their peers" (2000, p. 60).

When he shared his completed project with the class, he was met with some interesting questions. Here's part of that conversation:

AARON: Is stopping and getting fuel [part of your calculation]?

DEREK: I just figured the jets could keep going without any stops.

LAUREN: Did you start at the equator? If you flew to the equator, did you add that distance?

CHASE: If you flew around the equator it would never get dark.

DEREK: But if South Carolina was on the equator we'd still have night and day . . .

TEACHER: That's something we could investigate further. Is it possible to have sunlight on a place on the earth all day?

CRYSTAL: When did you start timing this: When the plane was on the ground, or when you started the motor, or when it was in the air?

DEREK: In the air. Just high enough to maybe . . . go over three houses.

KELVIN: Did you count the . . . National Day Line? Like if you passed that line it would be another day. Did you do that?

DEREK: Um . . .

TEACHER: Yes, there is a place called the International Date Line that marks where the day changes from one day to the next. Did you take that into consideration?

DEREK: Well, what I did was, it was just like a regular day. It was just like staying in South Carolina. This is one day. And tomorrow would be the next day . . .

COLE: Jets have to slow down when they refuel. Did you count that, when they have to slow down?

DEREK: Well, this is if it could go 350 miles per hour nonstop.

BRANDI: If they did try to refuel, and missed, they would have to be close to land, because they would almost be out of fuel. That's why they try to refuel when they're flying kind of low.

TEACHER: Brandi's inquiry project gave Derek a lot of basic information that he needed for his project.

DEREK: Yes, she gave me how high they can go, and the speeds. Say a hypersonic jet could go from 2,000 to 5,000 [miles per hour]. I did the middle number [3,500 mph].

TEACHER: Why did you do that?

DEREK: Because that's, well . . . if you went too fast . . . it's sort of like the average. It's in the middle.

CHRIS: If you were going in a jet, which way would it be going, the way the earth is rotating, or the other way?

DEREK: It wouldn't really matter. See, you could go either this way or that way [using the globe to show what he means]. It would probably take the same amount.

TEACHER: Although I know there can be differences. I know that when I've flown to California, there are certain winds that can slow the trip down, or speed it up if you are flying the other way.

DEREK: I was figuring it if you could go straight with no wind.

LAUREN: You could research how long it would take a hypersonic jet to go around the earth one million times.

It is worth reflecting on the significance of this conversation. Although the children had a lot of questions for Derek, they did not ask them in a critical or belittling way. Rather, they asked their questions in earnest because they wanted to better understand the assumptions that lay behind this data. The questions reflect the inquisitive, problem-posing nature of the class community. We had tried to encourage them to question numerical information, and their questions reflect this skeptical stance: When did you start timing? Did you include travel time to the equator? Did you count refueling time? Did you consider the International Date Line? Did you travel in the direction of the earth's rotation? Many of these questions Derek had not considered, but they helped him clarify his own thinking as well as offered other possible avenues to explore. From an inquiry perspective the attributes of a given problem, such as wind speed, refueling time, direction of flight, and so on, are not constraints that restrict our vision of the current problem. Instead, they serve as unique doorways for exploring future possibilities. They are helpful in framing where we are but also where we might want to go. This kind of classroom exchange reflects NCTM's Teaching Principle in which students are encouraged to raise questions, debate solutions, and justify results.

This conversation also highlighted the importance of the word *if*. Derek used the word *if* to overcome certain obstacles along the way; he knew the jets would need to be refueled but decided to reframe his problem by imagining, "What *if* they could go nonstop?" He knew that jets had a range of speeds but decided to pose the question, "What *if* they traveled at their middle speed?" Derek's classmates used these problem variables themselves to raise new questions, such as, If you traveled around the equator, would you remain in daylight throughout the trip? How long would it take a hypersonic jet to go around the earth one million times? From an inquiry perspective there is no neat and tidy point of closure when all our questions are answered; rather, there are always lingering questions to pursue.

Investigating the Fort McHenry Flag

Another mathematical investigation was prompted by a social studies discussion. The class had been studying the War of 1812 and was intrigued by the enormous size of the flag that flew over Fort McHenry: 42 feet long and 30 feet wide. The children had learned that Francis Scott Key, who was imprisoned on a faraway ship, could still see the flag because of its large size. It was this flag that later inspired him to write "The Star-Spangled Banner." Even though the children knew the dimensions of the flag, they still had difficulty imagining how large it really was. Robin suggested that someone might want to use math workshop time to develop a comparison that would help people better understand its dimensions.

As stated earlier in the chapter, the children were used to discussing mathematical comparisons in their reading, and now wanted to construct some of their own.

Bobby accepted the invitation. He had been fascinated by the size of the flag all along and was eager to compare it to more familiar objects. First he decided to mark off the length and the width of the flag in the hallway. He began by using rulers, and then realized that the 100-foot tape measure would make the task easier. Robin felt it was important for children to choose what tools they needed. She realized that she would be undermining their problem-solving efforts by telling them what materials to use. After this initial measuring Bobby wanted to compare the dimensions to something more familiar. He decided to compare these dimensions to three other different lengths: the heights of the class rabbit (Ellie), David W., and the tallest man in the world (as recorded in the latest *Guinness Book of World Records* (Cunningham 1992). His choices were certainly influenced by past explorations from the class community. Some children had used Ellie as a point of comparison during the pumpkin investigations earlier in the year. Also, David W. had shared several statistics (including the tallest man at 9 feet) from the *Guinness Book* as a way to intrigue children in its possibilities for investigation. Bobby had seen Chris and Kelvin use this same resource to devise a project around the largest potato chip in the world. So it is likely that Bobby drew upon all these ideas and then used them in a new context. To find his answers he measured David W. and Ellie and read about the tallest man. He then remeasured each of those lengths in the hallway as a way to compare them to the flag. He wrote in his journal: "If you add 9 of Dr. Whitins that is how long it would be. If the flag was 3 feet longer it will be 5 of the tallest man in the world ($9 \times 5 = 45 - 3 = 42$)." He chose to round off the height of David W. to 5 feet and found that almost 9 of those lengths reached 42 feet ($5 \times 9 = 45$). He later saw that extending the flag by another 3 feet would make it exactly 9 Davids long. He rounded off the height of the rabbit to 1 foot and easily tabulated the length of the flag to be 42 rabbits. The comparison was enlightening to Bobby. When he first measured David W. he said to him, "Gosh, you're pretty tall." However, after compiling his results, Bobby commented, "You know, Dr. Whitin isn't that tall at all!" Bobby was learning that all comparisons are relative, an important mathematical insight.

Next Bobby wanted to make a picture of his results. He knew his classmates needed a picture to better understand what he had found out. However, he was not sure how to start. He told Robin, "I want it to look right. You know, like a map or a model." Robin realized that Bobby wanted to know how to make the drawing proportionate. Bobby's desire to communicate and represent his findings to his peers in a meaningful way demonstrates several of NCTM's Process Standards for students (communication, representation). Robin felt that this was an appropriate time to give Bobby a minilesson on how to create a scale drawing. Embedding skills in a meaningful context makes more sense to students. Robin's direct instruction enabled Bobby to complete his picture for the class (Figure 6–6). Here again Robin was seeing more connections to what she had been doing in her reading and writing instruction. She was used to looking at a child's writ-

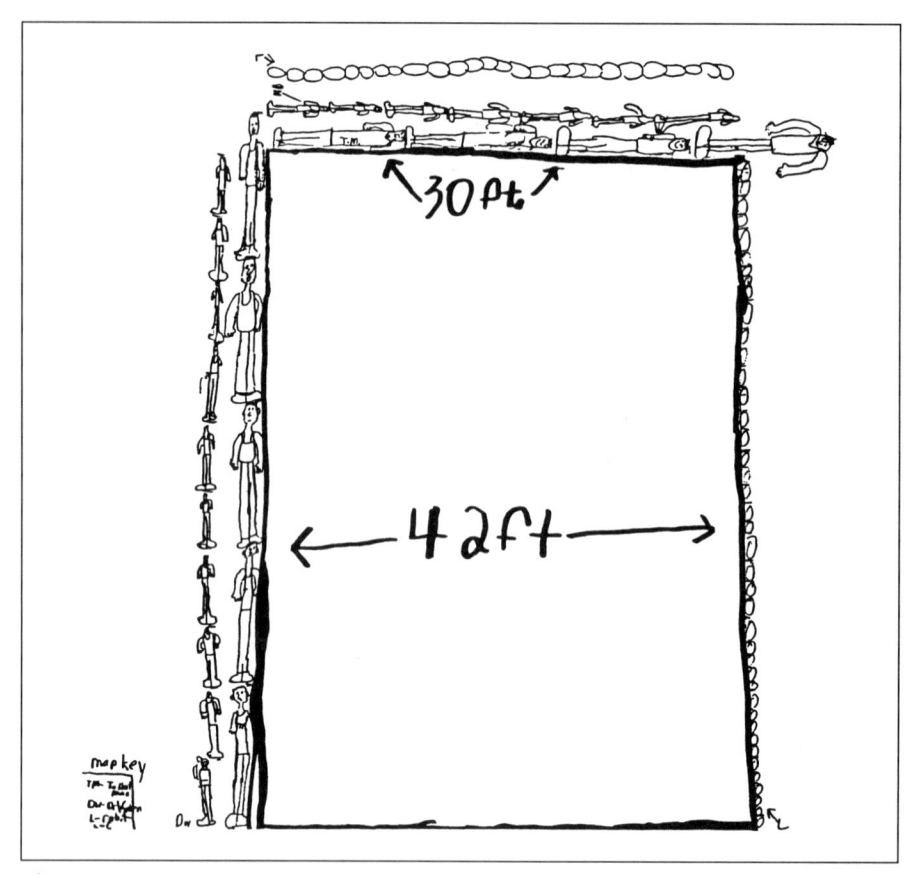

Figure 6–6

ing and giving a minilesson on the use of commas or quotation marks. As she listened to children discuss stories she was accustomed to giving minilessons to selected children on how to analyze plot or character development. She realized that her role in math workshop was no different. She knew she needed to continue to listen closely to her students and provide direct instruction when it was necessary and appropriate. This insight was an important turning point in Robin's understanding of the parallel between learning to write and learning to do mathematics. Direct instruction of skills, in both writing and math, makes more sense to students *and* teachers when it fulfills a need to communicate.

Counting to One Million

Erin, Chris, and Kelvin were intrigued with some of the statistics in *How Much Is a Million?* (Schwartz 1985) Robin knew of their interest and suggested that they might want to see if it really takes twenty-three days to count to one million (as

Schwartz calculates in his book). They decided to pursue this idea. They knew that larger numbers would take longer to say than smaller numbers, so they each counted to 100 using different starting points. They found the following results:

1–100	2 minutes
1,000–1,100	2 minutes, 15 seconds
10,000–10,100	3 minutes, 20 seconds
100,000–100,100	4 minutes, 15 seconds

They were unsure of how to incorporate these differing rates in their calculations. Instead, they used the first rate of 100 numbers per 2 minutes of counting to determine their answer. They constructed a chart that showed this functional relationship (Figure 6–7), finally tabulating 20,000 minutes to reach 1,000,000. Kelvin then reasoned how to convert the minutes to hours (and eventually days): "After 40 minutes comes 60 minutes (referring to his chart) and that's an hour. So then you just start your hours there. And then put 1 hour and 20 minutes (for 80 minutes), and then 1 hour and 40 minutes (for 100 minutes), and then we'll get it." As Erin continued her chart in this manner she noticed that when she reached the number 10,000 it took 3 hours and 20 minutes. We asked her, "Can you think of how this might help you to find out how long it would take you to count to 20,000?"

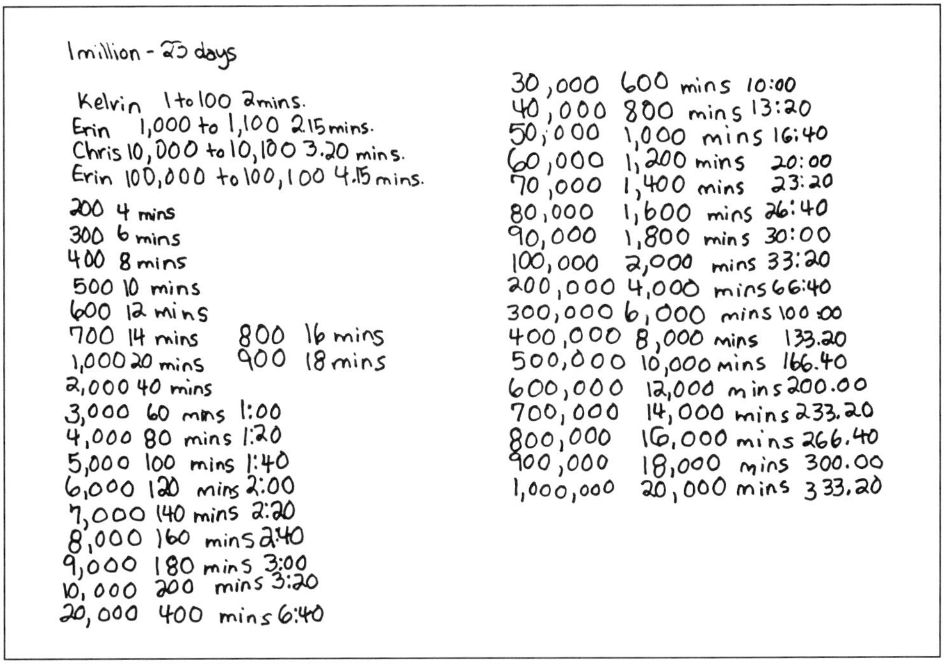

Figure 6–7

"Oh, it's just another 3 hours and 20 minutes. So that's 6 hours and . . . 40 minutes for 20,000." She used this doubling procedure to continue her calculations:

10,000	3 hours, 20 minutes
20,000	6 hours, 40 minutes
40,000	13 hours, 20 minutes
80,000	26 hours, 40 minutes

She realized that she did not want to double again because she was seeking to land on 100,000 (for easier counting to 1,000,000). Instead, she remembered that it took 200 minutes to reach 10,000. So she converted 200 minutes by using a calculator and successively subtracting 60 from 200:

200 − 60 = 1 hour
140 − 60 = 2 hours
80 − 60 = 3 hours
20 minutes remaining
Total: 3 hours and 20 minutes per 10,000 counting numbers

We later discussed with Erin how she could have used division to make the calculation more easily. However, by letting her use the calculator in her own way, she was able to see how division was really a process of repeated subtraction. Erin used this same subtraction process as she converted 2,000 minutes, the time to count to 100,000. She used this answer of 33 hours and 20 minutes to count on to 1,000,000. This problem gave her facility in using the calculator to convert these different units of time. Once the group reached 1,000,000 they wanted to convert their answer of 333 hours and 20 minutes to days so they could compare it more meaningfully to Schwartz's total of 23 days. Kelvin suggested using 24 hours and Erin elaborated, "Yes, so we could do 24 times 7 [uses calculator to find 168 hours]. Then we add 168 and 168 and that's . . . 336. Oh, 336 is too much [it's greater than the 333 hours of her total]. So minus 24 hours, that's 312 [336 − 24 = 312]." She knew that she was just shy of two weeks, so so reasoned, "That's 13 days. And 312 to 333 and 20 minutes is a leftover of 21 hours and 20 minutes. So that would be altogether, 13 days, 21 hours, and 20 minutes." The children reasoned that they must have counted more quickly than Schwartz. In reflecting on their project Chris thought about a logical extension to this project: "You know that first question on the chart, 'Who would find this information useful?' Well, we could write to David Schwartz and tell him how we got our answers and he might think it's interesting how we did this." It pleased us that Chris saw his project as important mathematical work and needed to be shared with others in the larger mathematical community. Part of the reason we included this question is that we wanted the children to think of audiences beyond their immediate classroom.

They did in fact write a letter to David M. Schwartz and received a reply (Figure 6–8). Schwartz nicely validated the children as mathematical thinkers. He emphasized strategies and ways of thinking about problems rather than a single right answer. He also nudged them to do some further recalculating to take into account different rates of counting. The children (and the rest of the class) saw this letter as noteworthy recognition for the important work they were doing in math workshop.

Other Math Workshop Explorations

In addition to works of children's literature, the ideas for math workshop projects came from other sources as well. Chase and Chris wanted to find out the hat sizes of people in the class. They developed this idea on a special school day called "Backwards Tacky Day," in which children wear odd pieces of clothing (often backwards). "Everyone was wearing hats that day and so I started to wonder what size they were wearing." His written reflection reminded us of the kind of mathematical viewing of the world that is embedded in *Counting on Frank.* We wanted to cultivate a habit of seeing the world through mathematical lenses and saw that math workshop was giving children time to carry out these mathematical musings. Chase and Chris measured hat size by the number of snaps needed to fit the hat on each person's head. They then calculated the mode (most frequently occurring) of hat sizes (5) and wrote in their journal: "A person who might find this interesting is maybe a person who sells fitted hats in the children's department so he can stock up on more hats of that size on the shelf." Thinking about an intended audience for his mathematical results is an effective way to operationalize NCTM's Communication Standard.

Several children developed projects using manipulatives. Cole used pattern blocks to investigate the number of pieces needed to make larger and larger versions of each shape; for example, how many squares are needed to make the next largest square. Robin suggested this idea and Cole decided to pursue it. We did offer possible ideas for exploration and, in hindsight, we probably should have done so more often. Children still were the ones who decided if they wanted to investigate the problem or change it in some way. Cole found, "If you keep hooking on diamonds [parallelograms] to diamonds it will always be a diamond. And squares make other squares. Everything works without the help of anything else [other shapes] except hexagons." His work (Figure 6–9) shows that he found the numerical pattern of 1, 4, 9, 16, 25, 36 . . . and described the differences among those numbers (3, 5, 7, 9, 11) as "adds 2 each time" and "skipping one number each time." Investigating each of these shapes was quite a time-consuming project for Cole, who commented to us, "You know, I've been working on this for a long time. Other people have started other projects, like plane speeds. But I'm still interested in doing this." We shared his reflection with the rest of the class to underscore his perseverance and autonomy as a problem solver. We tried to be alert to children's reflections about their problem-solving efforts and share them regularly

Dear Kelvin, Chris and Erin,

Thank you so much for your letter, your calculations, and that wonderful big book. I loved them all!

I am always delighted when children test the statements in my book, *How Much Is A Million?* When you do that, you are finding out what mathematics really is—a process of experiment and discovery, just like any other science. Yes, mathematics is a science! Fortunately, it's a lot more than just memorization of multiplication facts and solving problems about apples and oranges or change from the store.

The question that you tackled—how long would it take to count from one to one million—has many answers, not just the one I put in my book. You discovered an answer for yourself, which makes me happy. Because my answer was 23 days and yours was a little under 14 days, it doesn't mean one of us is right and one is wrong. After all, people count at different rates of speed, just as people run at different rates of speed.

The difference between your answer and mine is partially explained because you counted at a faster rate. There is another explanation, too. I tried to account for the fact that as the numbers get bigger they take longer to say. I know that you were aware of that, because you found it took 2 minutes to count from 1 to 100, 2.15 minutes to count from 1,000 to 1,100, 3.2 minutes to count from 10,000 to 10,100, and 4.15 minutes to count from 100,000 to 100,100. In each of these cases, you counted 100 numbers, but it took more than twice as long to count them when they were over 100,000 than when they were under 100.

But I noticed that in your calculation, you did not allow for this difference in counting rates as the numbers get bigger. You counted at the same rate (2 minutes for every 100 numbers) all the way up to one million. Since 90% (or nine-tenths) of the numbers between one an one million are higher than 100,000, you might want to ask yourself if a speed of 2 minutes per 100 numbers is the most accurate way to estimate the answer. Perhaps it would be more accurate to call 4 minutes per 100 numbers the average speed.

I must tell you once again that there is no right answer to this question. There are different strategies for answering the question, and you picked a very good one. But after you think some more about it, you might decide to pick an even better one. That's for *you* to decide, not me!

I also want to point out that a calculation like this is extremely difficult! You are very courageous to attempt it at all. The mathematics of changing values (which is what we have here) is called calculus, and normally students study calculus in college. So you are doing college math! Congratulations!!!

I'm enclosing three copies of a picture, which I have autographed, and three bookmarks. I hope you enjoy them.

Keep on reading and keep on experimenting with math!

A million good wishes,

David M. Schwartz

Figure 6–8

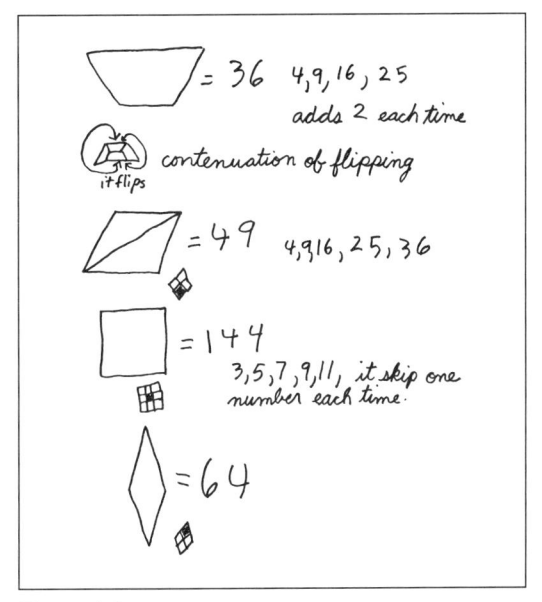

Figure 6–9

with the class so that together we developed a healthy set of attitudes and dispositions about mathematical learning.

Derek used the geoboard and the strategy of problem posing to set new directions for himself. He made one design (Figure 6–10) and then listed its attributes and possible extensions. He looked at all his options and decided to use attributes 1 and 6 to pose his next challenge: "Could I make a design that looked the same all the time using two trapezoids and using all but one peg?" His phrase "looked the same all the time" referred to the idea of rotational symmetry. He wanted to build a design that could be rotated 90 degrees and look the same as its original orientation. He found that this investigation was not possible because of his stipulation about pegs. However, he was able to make a large hexagon from two trapezoids, and he saw it had rotational symmetry. We teachers had demonstrated this strategy of listing attributes and extensions in several other activities we did together as a class earlier in the year. We reminded the class that they could use this strategy themselves to help them create new problems from a given problem. We wanted the children to see that from an inquiry perspective investigations are never really finished. We were seeing that in math workshop children could demonstrate this important idea to each other in many different contexts.

Teachers' Reflections on Math Workshop: Benefits and Next Steps

As we reflected on our experience with math workshop, we recalled several benefits. We saw that this time provided interdisciplinary connections: Bobby realized anew just how big that flag was during the Revolutionary War; Hedda learned

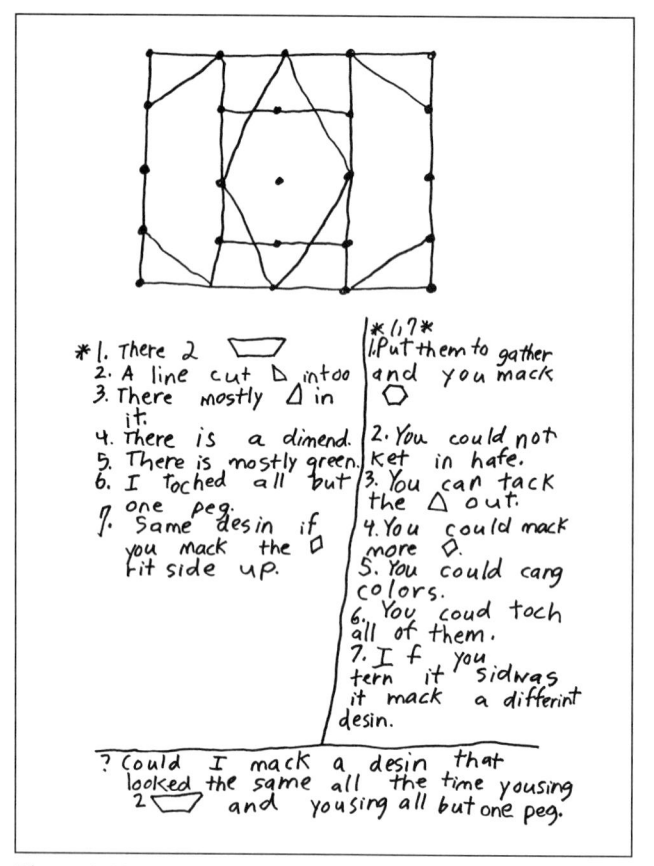

Figure 6–10

some lessons about marketing and economics as she investigated how to increase profits at the school store; and Lauren learned some lessons about phone etiquette as she called a local radio station to report her findings about favorite television shows. Math workshop also demonstrated to us the importance of learning math concepts in a meaningful context. Bobby learned about ratio in doing his scale drawing; Jake learned about rounding in calculating the number of points scored in a basketball season; and Jennifer learned about averaging as she calculated the average height of a fifth grader. Despite these benefits, we thought about changes we would make to this workshop time in future years. These modifications included the following:

1. Look for opportunities to conduct minilessons on math concepts and skills that the children encounter. For instance, several children were interested in calculating averages. Robin wanted to be more aware of

the support the children needed so she could conduct minilessons on topics that were relevant to them. Robin was used to conducting minilessons during writing workshop about writer's craft, such as lead sentences and descriptive verbs, as well as common grammar or punctuation errors. She saw that she could use the expertise that she had developed in writing workshop to assist her students in their mathematical learning.

2. Highlight the diversity of ways that children represent their mathematical ideas. We could have made large charts that summarized the different ways that children wrote about and drew their findings. We realized that we could have encouraged children to use graphs more often to represent their data. If we made public these different forms of representation, then children would have more ideas for communicating their own findings.

3. Look for more math topics throughout the day. For instance, Robin wanted to capitalize on the questions the children raised in social studies and science and extend them into mathematical invitations. We thought about posting an ongoing chart of math workshop questions as another way to foster a mathematical habit of mind.

4. List possible extensions and unanswered questions for each person's project. We realized that it is important not only to celebrate each person's insights but also to list possible next steps. In this way children can have more ideas to draw upon as they search for another math topic to investigate.

5. Keep better track of how long each child is spending on a topic. As in any classroom, some children use their time better than others. Robin kept a "status of the class" list of children's names and their projects, but we realized afterward that we needed to examine it more closely. Some children spent too much time on a project because they were not using their time wisely. We also felt that we needed to leave the last ten to twelve minutes for uninterrupted writing to insure that everyone recorded their thoughts and reflections each day.

Children's Reflections on the Benefits of Math Workshop

Robin always tried to inform children explicitly about her curricular decisions. On this occasion Robin explained that she had decided to offer math workshop time to the class because she wanted them to have some choice in the mathematics they explored. She then asked each child to respond in their journal to this question: "Do you think it is a good idea for the class to have a choice of what to do during math workshop time? Why or why not?" Their responses eloquently captured some of the important attitudes and dispositions that she was striving to foster in her mathematical community.

HEDDA: I think it's a good idea to let us decide what we want to explore because everyone has different interests than Ms. Cox. We can also choose [whether] we want to work in groups or individually.

COLE: I think the inevitable problems that [we would face] when we got older will be easier if we had math workshop. Because we have found out the way to solve problems now.

CHRIS B.: I think people would work harder and it would be more fun if someone did something that they wanted rather than have someone tell them what they have to do. I also think it would make someone go the extra mile to get things done right. I think that, in a way, it is preparing us for the real world because in most things we have the option to say either "yes" or "no." It would also help us make important decisions.

CHRIS F.: When we get to choose we will probably do more investigating on our question.

TALITHA: At first when Ms. Cox told us about math workshop I just was surprised. I never knew teachers would or could do this. Math workshop is a fun time for me. I'm glad that we can choose what we want to do. If Ms. Cox chose what we did, someone might not like it. If they don't, then they don't learn or listen, which is bad. Now that we chose what we want to learn we are able to pay attention to others because they are usually very interesting.

ERIN: It was the right decision because it lets us explore what we want to and we can work with other people.

RICHIE: It lets us feel like we did the whole project ourselves.

LAUREN: I like Ms. Cox's decision because: (1) Nobody does the same thing. This means that we all get to do something different. That way it's more exciting. (2) We all learn neat things. This means that we can look at different people's findings and how they concluded this. It's more educating . . . (3) We understand what we're doing. This means we know what's going on. We also learn a lot by doing it ourselves. We learn from our findings and mistakes.

Their comments reflect many of the attitudes of problem solvers that NCTM seeks to promote. For instance, children see that math workshop increases their confidence in themselves as mathematicians. They learn from their own investigations and even from their own mistakes. We had tried hard to promote the attitude that mistakes are opportunities for further reflection and personal growth. Robin used several strategies in this regard: (1) She read pieces of literature that highlighted the value of mistakes. One example is *Mistakes That Worked* (Jones 1994), which describes how unanticipated results led to new discoveries. (2) She viewed mistakes as interesting data to inquire about, not as something to be embarrassed about: "Let's look at this answer and try to investigate the thinking behind it." (3) She explained to children why she was devoting class time to examining mistakes: "Mistakes are examples of sense making just as much as correct solutions. As problem solvers we are all trying to make sense of a given situation. We are a class that is always thinking. Mistakes are just another way to think about our thinking." (4) She asked children to write a reflection in their journal about what they had learned during a discussion of a mistake. In this way the children become more reflective about the benefits of examining all kinds of thinking.

The children also noted that choice granted them a sense of ownership and responsibility for completing the task. They remarked that they developed a more personal investment in the project because they enjoyed the freedom to choose. They saw the relevance of their work because the skills and attitudes they were using were beneficial not only to the present task, but also to other problems that they would encounter. They were more eager to listen, as a community, to the work of others because of the diversity of investigations and the personal investment that was a part of all their projects. Last, their opportunity to choose put the focus on understanding. They were the ones who initiated the investigation and they were the ones who bore the responsibility for communicating their results to themselves and their peers. For these many reasons, we felt that math workshop helped us in developing a collaborative mathematical community. It benefited the individual student as well as the entire class.

7 Reflections on Living a Mathematical Life

At the end of the year we asked the children to write a reflection on what it means to think mathematically. We asked them to cite mathematical thinkers if they wished, and to draw upon any experiences and discussions that we had as a class during the year.

Chris commented on the importance of the "what if" phrase that he first encountered in *Counting on Frank* (Clement 1991). He wrote: "Frank's master is a mathematical thinker. Therefore, they use 'what if.' 'What ifs' kind of spiff up a project . . . 'What if' is a powerful word because it propels our questions. It opens our minds and thoughts to new horizons, and therefore we ask very interesting questions! It allows us to explore projects that are really impossible. Example: Derek's jet that flies around the world." David M. Schwartz, who uses the word *if* in many of his books, has also commented on the importance of this word (Whitin and Wilde 1995, p. 124):

> I would say [when I was younger], What would I find if I could go to the end of the universe? What would be there? As if it were a yard or something. Would there be a brick wall there, with a sign that says, Do not go beyond this point? "If" allows you to violate all the assumptions of the universe, of our life, and of our thought processes. It takes you into other worlds mentally.

So part of living a mathematical life is playing with mathematical possibilities, and the word *if* nurtures that mental inquisitiveness.

Derek emphasized the importance of persistence and sense making. He recalled his project on the jet: "I had to decide what numbers to divide or multiply. Like to divide 350 [mph] by 38 inches [distance around the model globe], or 25,080 [miles around the earth] by 350. I knew that 350 had to be in there somewhere because it was the speed of the jet. So I decided to go with 25,080/350 because that is how many miles it is around the earth. Sometimes I divided the wrong things, and I knew it was either too big or too small. If you want to be a mathematical thinker, or you are one, then you should remember to never give up."

Derek also mentioned the importance of raising additional questions: "Another thing that mathematical thinkers should remember is that even when they get an answer, that there is more and more answers to that question. It could be different with different jets and different speeds." Derek knew that he could generate a variety of answers by changing some of the variables of his problem. Jake commented on this same idea: "A mathematical thinker is calculating stuff, like how many steps will it take if I walk to a place. Well, it depends on how big of a step you take." He underscored the critical disposition of questioning answers, and exposing the assumptions behind a given statement. Michael connected this skeptical attitude by giving an example from *How Much Is a Million?* (Schwartz 1985): "Mathematical thinkers think that there are two answers to some problems. In the book *How Much Is a Million?* they say that a whale weighs as much as a million quarters, but they don't say *what kind* of whale. There can be many answers to this question because there are many different kinds of whales."

Several children commented on the social context in which mathematical thinkers find themselves. Brandon wrote: "A mathematical thinker is someone who studies math and just enjoys working with people who are excited about mathematical things." Being with colleagues who are interested in exploring ideas is a powerful attraction for people who want to think and grow in their mathematical understanding. Lindsay G. also affirmed this social dimension of learning: "Mathematical thinkers ask for other peoples' opinions about something and compare them with their ideas. Some people might think differently [than you] and share with you what they think. I think that someone who shares with the whole class, and not just with their friends, is a good thinker." Lindsay sees what Vygotsky (1978) has observed, that is, that we outgrow our current understandings with the help of others.

Ruth wrote specifically about how mathematical thinkers use the ideas of others to generate new thoughts of their own: "Mathematical thinkers wonder what other people think, and get another idea every time something else is mentioned." Melissa B. affirmed how mathematical thinkers delay judgment until they have considered the ideas of their peers: "Mathematical thinkers don't just base [their answers] on just what they think, and then try to solve it. They get other peoples' ideas too and see what they think. They see what is really the best answer." Melissa E. observed that mathematical thinkers think about their daily events in mathematical terms, and she learned this idea from one of her peers: "Someone who is a mathematical thinker thinks about questions from things around them. For example, they could ask questions about trees, grass, cars, or anything. I was thinking about how Jason could ask questions about anything. He was just asking questions about stuff around him. He could get a question out of just about anything." Like Frank's owner, Melissa was seeing the relevance of mathematics in the world around her.

A Conversation with Jason

More than anyone else, Jason exhibited a mathematical frame of mind. Melissa and others recognized that thinking and learned important lessons from him. Jason wrote in his final reflection:

I think a mathematical thinker is someone who looks at most everything he sees and thinks, I wonder how I could relate this to math.

A mathematical thinker wants to go beyond the boundaries of just finding something out.

A mathematical thinker wants to explore more about why, where, when, what and how. I think those phrases are the most powerful phrases in math.

Mathematical thinkers *want* to find out more.
They just don't do it for extra credit.

One last thing, I think a mathematical thinker realizes that math is an everyday process, and is willing to use his skills anytime.

We interviewed Jason later on and asked him to explain some of these ideas further. We were intrigued with his phrase "going beyond the boundaries" and wanted him to say more about that: "Well, what I mean by that is that I think a mathematical thinker doesn't just want to say, 'OK, 2 plus 2 equals 4, or 8 times 8 is 64.' They don't just want to find out and write it down. They think about, How did multiplication come to be? I need to find this out. I need to get the information to other people." When we asked him if he could give an example of going beyond the boundaries from this past year, he replied, "We did this fraction thing with ½ of this or that. We got into three-dimensional shapes, other shapes, pie graphs, and other things, instead of just ½ is ½." Jason was one who kept extending investigations. He was the one who wondered if fractions applied to other noncircular shapes, including three-dimensional ones. He was the one who wondered if the 3:1 ratio of the circumference to the diameter could apply to other shapes. It was Jason who wondered if there was a base 11 (which led others to explore other base blocks that were available in the room). His questioning was a powerful demonstration to others about what it means to think mathematically.

We asked Jason to explain what "wondering" meant to him: "A wonder is used very highly in math. I use it highly; people in here use it a lot. Like a math problem, 8 times 8 is 64. After 64 . . . mathematical thinkers say, I wonder why . . . What I am saying is, the answer isn't really the answer to most mathematical thinkers . . . The answer is research, after research, after research . . . The answer is just the beginning, the answer is just the beginning."

We were also curious about Jason's perspective on our role as teachers in the classroom. We asked open-ended questions throughout the year, and it became evident that we did not know the answers to some of the questions the children were posing. We often did some further work ourselves, or consulted with other colleagues, and reported back to the children on questions they had posed. Jason noticed this stance we took as inquirers, and talked about teachers as learners: "Teachers who think they are supposed to know all the answers are not mathematical thinkers. Because they probably just looked in the book, and found it out, and stopped there. Memorized it and just stopped. They are not mathematical thinkers who just find it out, act like they know everything, and just stop . . . And if you have a teacher who is not a mathematical thinker, that doesn't mean you can't be one. The teacher doesn't run your life. You can. Once you set your mind to it, you can be anything you'd like to be." His comments helped us realize again the important role that teachers play in demonstrating mathematical inquisitiveness. As teachers we teach more than content. We teach attitudes about learning. It is an interesting irony that the more we take risks ourselves as teachers, opening ourselves up to the unexpected and sometimes the unanswerable, the more we also give confidence to our students. In our own vulnerability we strengthen others.

A Mathematician's Bill of Rights

The children's reflections about what it means to think mathematically conjured up for us a Bill of Rights for mathematical thinkers. Although we did not create this document with the students, we would want to do so in the future. This Bill of Rights captures many of the children's comments, and certainly reflects the attributes of mathematical communities advocated by NCTM.

A Mathematician's Bill of Rights

As a mathematician I have the right to:

Pose my own questions
Create, revise, and abandon hypotheses
Hear and reflect on the thinking of my peers
Initiate my own investigations
Share my rough-draft thinking
Solve problems in ways that make sense to me
Question the reasons behind the procedures
Investigate the unexpected
Be skeptical of numerical information
Describe and define mathematical ideas in my own language
Build on the ideas of my peers
Represent my ideas in many different ways
Capitalize on mistakes as sites for learning
Challenge ideas in a respectful way
Learn about the history of mathematical ideas and language
Solve a problem in more than one way

However, we do not conclude this book with the Bill of Rights. As Jason said, inquirers keep asking questions. So we saved the last word for Melissa:

> I still want to find out,
> Really, just about anything,
> Because there is still so much
> To find out.

References

Biesty, Stephen. 1993. *Man-of-War: Stephen Biesty's Cross-Sections*. New York: DK Publishing.

Brown, Stephen I., and Marion Walter. 1990. *The Art of Problem Posing*. Mahwah, NJ: Lawrence Erlbaum.

Clement, Rod. 1991. *Counting on Frank*. Milwaukee: Gareth Stevens.

Cole, Joanna. 1985. *Large as Life Animals*. New York: Knopf.

Cunningham, Antonia, ed. 1992. *The Guinness Book of World Records*. New York: Bantam.

Darling, David. 1991. *Spiderwebs to Skyscrapers: The Science of Structure*. New York: Dillon Press.

Davis, Robert. 1964. *Discovery in Mathematics: A Text for Teachers*. Reading, MA: Addison-Wesley.

Drew, David. 1989. *The Book of Animal Records*. Crystal Lake, IL: Heinemann Library.

Gallas, Karen. 1994. *The Languages of Learning: How Children Talk, Write, Dance, Draw, and Sing Their Understanding of the World*. New York: Teachers College Press.

Grifalconi, Ann. 1986. *The Village of Round and Square Houses*. Boston: Little, Brown.

Heaton, Ruth M. 2000. *Teaching Mathematics to the New Standards: Relearning the Dance*. New York: Teachers College Press.

Heymann, Tom. 1992. *In an Average Lifetime . . .* New York: Fawcett Columbine.

Hiebert, James, et al. 1997. *Making Sense: Teaching and Learning Mathematics with Understanding*. Portsmouth, NH: Heinemann.

Jones, Charlotte Foltz. 1994. *Mistakes That Worked*. New York: Doubleday.

Lasky, Katherine. 1997. *The Most Beautiful Roof in the World: Exploring the Rainforest Canopy*. San Diego: Harcourt Brace.

Macaulay, David. 1973. *Cathedral: The Story of Its Construction*. Boston: Houghton Mifflin.

———. 1980. *Unbuilding*. Boston: Houghton Mifflin.

Mills, Heidi, Timothy O'Keefe, and David Whitin. 1996. *Mathematics in the Making: Authoring Ideas in Primary Classrooms*. Portsmouth, NH: Heinemann.

Morris, Ann. 1992. *Houses and Homes*. New York: Lothrop, Lee and Shepard.

National Council of Teachers of Mathematics. 1989. *Curriculum and Evaluation Standards for School Mathematics*. Reston, VA: NCTM.

———. 1991. *Professional Standards for Mathematics Teaching*. Reston, VA: NCTM.

———. 2000. *Principles and Standards for School Mathematics*. Reston, VA: NCTM.

Ross, Catherine Sheldrick. 1992. *Circles: Shapes in Math, Science and Nature*. Reading, MA: Addison Wesley.

———. 1994. *Triangles: Shapes in Math, Science and Nature*. Toronto: Kids Can Press.

———. 1996. *Squares: Shapes in Math, Science and Nature*. Toronto: Kids Can Press.

Rubenstein, Rheta. 1996. "Strategies to Support the Learning of the Language of Mathematics." In *Communication in Mathematics, K–12 and Beyond*, ed. Portia C. Elliott, 214–218. Reston, VA: NCTM.

Rubenstein, Rheta, and R. Schwartz. 2000. "Word Histories: Melding Mathematics and Meaning." *Mathematics Teacher* 93 (November): 664–669.

Schillereff, Mary. 2001. "Using Inquiry-Based Science to Help Gifted Students Become More Self-Directed." *Primary Voices* 10(1): 28–32.

Schoenfeld, Alan, ed. 1994. *Mathematical Thinking and Problem Solving*. Hillsdale, NJ: Lawrence Erlbaum.

Schwartz, David M. 1985. *How Much Is a Million?* New York: Lothrop, Lee and Shepard.

———. 1989. *If You Made a Million*. New York: Lothrop, Lee and Shepard.

Scieszka, Jon. 1995. *Math Curse*. New York: Viking.

Short, Kathy, Jerome Harste, and Carolyn Burke. 1996. *Creating Classrooms for Authors and Inquirers*, 2d ed. Portsmouth, NH: Heinemann.

Vygotsky, Lev. 1978. *Mind in Society*. Cambridge, MA: Harvard University Press.

Walter, Marion. 1970. "A Common Misconception about Area." *Arithmetic Teacher* (September): 286–289.

Watson, Dorothy, Carolyn Burke, and Jerome Harste. 1989. *Whole Language: Inquiring Voices*. New York: Scholastic.

Whitin, David J. 1993. "Viewing the World from a Mathematical Perspective." *Arithmetic Teacher* (April): 438–441.

Whitin, David, Heidi Mills, and Timothy O'Keefe. 1990. *Living and Learning Mathematics: Stories and Strategies for Supporting Mathematical Literacy*. Portsmouth, NH: Heinemann.

Whitin, David, and Sandra Wilde. 1992. *Read Any Good Math Lately? Children's Books for Mathematical Learning, K–6*. Portsmouth, NH: Heinemann.

———. 1995. *It's the Story That Counts: More Children's Books for Mathematical Learning, K–6*. Portsmouth, NH: Heinemann.

Whitin, Phyllis, and David Whitin. 2000. *Math Is Language Too: Talking and Writing in the Mathematics Classroom*. Urbana, IL: NCTE and Reston, VA: NCTM.

Wilkinson, Philip. 1993. *Amazing Buildings*. New York: Dorling Kindersley.

Wilson, Forrest. 1988. *What It Feels Like to Be a Building*. Washington, DC: Preservation Press.

Woodward, Virginia, and Wayne Serebrin. 1989. "Reading Between the Signs: The Social Semiotics of Collaborative Story Reading." *Linguistics and Education* 1: 393–414.

Yackel, Erma, and Paul Cobb. 1996. "Sociomathematical Norms, Argumentation, and Autonomy in Mathematics." *Journal for Research in Mathematics Education* 27: 458–477.

Zaslavsky, Claudia. 1989. "People Who Live in Round Houses." *Arithmetic Teacher* (September): 18–21.

———. 1994. *Multicultural Math*. New York: Scholastic.

———. 1996. *The Multicultural Math Classroom: Bringing in the World*. Portsmouth, NH: Heinemann.

Additional Trade Books about Architecture

Crosbie, Michael. 2000. *Arches to Zigzags: An Architecture ABC*. New York: Abrams.

Jordan, Sandra, and Jan Greenberg. 2000. *Frank O. Gehry: Outside In*. New York: DK Publishing.

Kaner, Etta. 1994. *Bridges*. Toronto: Kids Can Press.

Macaulay, David. 2000. *Building Big*. Boston: Houghton Mifflin.

Mann, Elizabeth. 1996. *The Brooklyn Bridge*. New York: Mikaya Press.

Murphy, Pat. 1993. *By Nature's Design*. San Francisco: Chronicle Books.

Sturges, Philemon. 1998. *Bridges Are to Cross*. New York: Puffin.

Thorne-Thomsen, Kathleen. 1994. *Frank Lloyd Wright for Kids*. Chicago: Chicago Review Press.